Moving Through a Sacred Place

Rocky Mountain Books

The Whaleback

A Walking Guide
by Bob Blaxley

Moving Through a Sacred Place

Limber pine pictures on pages 1, 9, 25, 37, 43 & 85 by Gillean Daffern.

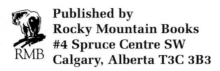
Published by
Rocky Mountain Books
#4 Spruce Centre SW
Calgary, Alberta T3C 3B3

The publisher gratefully acknowledges the
assistance provided by the Alberta
Foundation for the Arts and by the federal
Department of Canadian Heritage.

COMMITTED TO THE DEVELOPMENT OF CULTURE AND THE ARTS

Canadian Cataloguing in Publication Data

Blaxley, Bob, 1953-
  The Whaleback

  ISBN 0-921102-56-9

  1. Whaleback Ridge Region (Alta.)--Guidebooks. 2. Hiking--
Alberta--Whaleback Ridge Region--Guidebooks. 3. Trails--
Alberta--Whaleback Ridge Region--Guidebooks. I. Title. II.
Title: Moving through a sacred place.
GV199.44.C22W52 1997   917.123'4   C97-910282-0

Contents

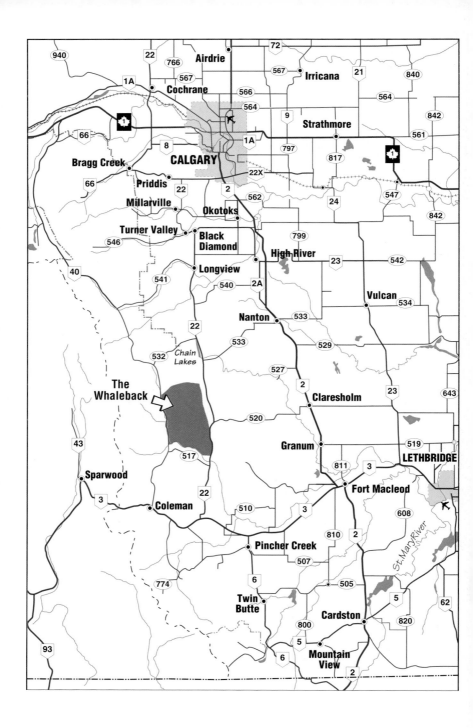

Introduction

*I*n Alberta, public policy and environmental advocacy groups recognize the importance of public input into conservation matters. In the area of wildland protection, many factors are involved but environmental activists are keenly aware that an active, vocal constituency of support is a key ingredient for preserving the natural values of a particular area. Developing this constituency is often problematic for two major reasons:

- Many recreational users of a wild area who would support its preservation are unaware of threats to its ecological integrity or issues surrounding protection.
- Many undesignated wilderness areas receive low visitation because people who are not residents in the area do not know how to gain access, nor do they know possible areas where it is appropriate to walk.

People with a direct knowledge of, and connection to, a natural area are the logical members of any preservation oriented constituency. However, surmounting the above issues has been difficult for organizations devoted to preserving wilderness. A guidebook oriented toward preservation of the country described would help to bridge this gap between recreational users and conservationists.

The Whaleback area of southwestern Alberta is an essentially roadless region of rare montane landscape. At present it has no formal protected status but is a candidate area under the province's Special Places 2000 program. Proposals to drill an exploratory well for oil and natural gas in the area led to a widely publicized hearing in the spring of 1994. At that time many people became concerned about the area's protection as a result of publicity surrounding the hearings. However, with the decision of the Energy Resources Conservation Board disallowing the exploratory well, the area has received much less notice.

Many people who are active hikers in areas such as nearby Kananaskis Country and Banff and Waterton national parks and who are interested in conservation do not know the location of the Whaleback, how to gain access or routes to follow once there. The majority of people who are using the area now are hunters in the fall and off-road-vehicle (ORV) enthusiasts in the summer. The Friends of the Whaleback, a group dedicated to preserving the natural values of the region, have identified the need for a guidebook giving people access and route information for the area.

Trail guides are a common genre in the literature on wilderness. There are literally hundreds of them for natural areas in North America and they tend to be very similar in layout and content. Most are descriptive, giving detailed directions to trail heads and the routes to be followed while walking. A substantial percentage also include information on the human and natural history of the area they cover. Very few guidebooks focus in any way on preservation issues in the natural areas described.

The Whaleback area has no signage or guidebook indicating access and routes. It also does not have a large constituency of people who regularly use the countryside and are aware of the conservation issues pertaining to it. In order to remedy these shortcomings I decided to write a walking guide that would include a focus on preservation of the area.

In compiling this guidebook I interviewed individuals concerned with the area, conducted a review of pertinent literature and walked all of the routes at least once during the spring and summer of 1996. The location of the routes and features described on them were checked using a Global Positioning System receiver. Other routes were walked in the course of the research but were not included for a variety of reasons, mostly centred on access difficulties.

The guidebook will assist people in gaining access to the area and give them the information necessary to appreciate and steward it. It should also help to expand the constituency that will support preservation initiatives and oppose industrial development of the area. Given that wild areas are becoming more scarce in this increasingly crowded world and that urban dwellers are continuing to seek recreation in pristine natural areas, it appears inevitable that the Whaleback area will experience increased visitor use in the future. By developing a guidebook that stresses the importance of minimum impact practices and the preservation of the area's natural wild qualities, I hope that the community of concerned advocates with an ethos of stewardship will be enlarged and fostered.

Acknowledgements

I would like to express my gratitude to Dr. Stephen Herrero who was my supervisor for the Master's Degree project that resulted in this book, to Professor Michael Robinson, Executive Director, Arctic Institute of North America, for spending many hours sharing his experience in writing and publishing and his enthusiasm for preserving wilderness and to Professor Brenda Naylor, Faculty of Environmental Design, for many hours of assistance in editing the manuscript. I am also indebted to Bryon Benn (consultant in prairie restoration) and Ross Hastings (curator of botany at the Provincial Museum of Alberta) for their invaluable ecological knowledge and help. Finally to my daughter, Anna Blaxley, for her illustrations of fir and pine cones. The Faculty of Environmental Design at the University of Calgary supported my research with several scholarships for which I am extremely thankful.

Introduction to the Whaleback

The Montane Landscape

Every landscape has the power to evoke thought, emotion and action. Many people view areas such as mountains and deserts as extremes, bleak and inhospitable, while others view these same landscapes as exotic escapes from a banal, mundane existence. In modern times wilderness has become associated with extremes. Deep canyons, mountains, deserts; these are the places chosen today as representing the wild. Not long ago this was not the case; there were wild places that were more hospitable and welcoming to humans.

The Whaleback montane is a wild landscape that welcomes people. The original landscape the human species evolved in was probably savanna and there is much that speaks of home for modern humans in a place characterized by grasslands interspersed with patches of trees. In the southern Whaleback area there are extensive prairies composed of grasses and flowers. Where the soil conditions and aspect combine favourably there are patches of trees that extend fingers of forest into this prairie. As you move from south to north and east to west through the region trees start to predominate and the landscape becomes primarily a forest interspersed with meadows.

Walking through this landscape is often a delightful experience. The sky is typically clear, and when cloudy, the formations of the clouds are complex and interesting owing to the influence of strong winds around the Gap. The extreme variability of the country means that new types of forest or grassland are continually being encountered while scenic vistas can be dramatically revealed by turning a corner in a valley or topping a ridge. The variability in landscape also translates into a wide diversity of plants and animals present in this region. Many of the trails in the area are along valley bottoms and are suitable for people of all ages and levels of hiking ability.

The diversity of this landscape creates a wide variety of contact points between different plant communities, known as "ecotones" where numerous types of plants and animals can find favourable living conditions. The unique geographical position of the area contributes to this variety. The Whaleback is located at the juncture of three major different natural regions. On the northern edge vegetation associated with the foothills predominates. Coming up from the southeast a wide swath of prairie ascends the broad valley of the Oldman River. The western edge of the region is part of the Livingstone Range of the Rocky Mountains. Plants and animals from all three of these regions can find suitable living conditions in the Whaleback montane area.

The climate of the Whaleback area is strongly influenced by the presence of the Livingstone Gap, a steep-sided valley cut through the wall of the Livingstone Range. "The Gap" is in the southwest corner of the Whaleback area. It was created by the ancient Oldman River during the time the Rockies were eroding from the plateau created by a tectonic uplift about 70 million years ago. The Gap allows warm dry chinook winds to enter the Whaleback area, and because the mountain barrier is lower around the Gap, warm chinook winds from the Pacific flow through it earlier and stay longer than they do along other parts of the Eastern Slopes. These warm dry winds are responsible for the conditions that allow the montane to flourish in the vicinity of the southern end of the Whaleback Ridge. (See photograph on page 18.)

The classic montane landscape includes grasslands, limber pine and Douglas fir forests, lodgepole pine forests and white spruce forests. Aspect plays a critical role in determining where different forests and grasslands will grow. In the southern portion of the Whaleback area, north- and east-facing slopes tend to have closed Douglas fir forests if the slope is well drained. Lower on these slopes there are extensive aspen stands. On north-facing slopes around springs and streams white spruce forests are common. In some areas open lodgepole pine forests are found on North facing slopes instead of Douglas fir. It appears that these lodgepole pine forests are the first trees to establish themselves following a forest fire.

The ridge top forests are generally a mixture of limber pine and Douglas fir and tend to be open with grasses and low shrubs as the understory. Grasslands dominate the south- and west-facing slopes of the southern part of the area, often extending to the ridge crests.

A noteworthy attribute of this region is the presence of extensive areas of willow shrubland in the broad valley bottoms of Bob Creek and Breeding Valley. Low willow/swamp birch communities are relatively rare in montane regions, but there are extensive patches in these areas.

The unique conditions present in the Whaleback montane make it a place that permits the most northern or southern occurrence for many species. There are estimated to be over 80 species of birds that breed in the Whaleback area and many other species use the area when migrating. Montane

Douglas fir near Camp Creek.

is a particularly good habitat for songbirds, rivalling the best areas in North America for diversity. One of the most significant aspects of the Whaleback montane region vis-à-vis wildlife is its status as one of the most significant elk wintering grounds in Alberta. During the months of December through May up to 2,000 elk use the area for winter grazing.

11

Ancient limber pine on Little Whaleback Ridge.

In winter these elk and other animals in the area are often balanced on the edge of survival. The "energy budget" for elk in winter is very close to being balanced *without* human disturbance. If they are disturbed by too much human activity during the months of December through April, it is possible they will not be able to take enough time to eat sufficient grass to keep them strong until spring. For this reason, it is important that people walking in the area during the winter confine themselves to trails along the valley bottoms. If you see elk ahead of you and your presence might disturb them, or if they appear restless or frightened, turn around and go back. If you must get past, give them as wide a detour as you can. These actions can quite literally make a life or death difference to these animals.

The southeast corner of the Whaleback area.

Ecological processes such as fire and insect infestation have profound effects on landscapes. These interconnected processes operate differently in various vegetation communities and stages of their growth and can be strongly influenced by climatic factors. These processes have been altered and suppressed in the Whaleback area since European settlement.

When the first ranches were established in this area the countryside was much more open. This was probably owing to frequent burning. A discussion of fire and insect suppression in this area and some implications is found in the chapter "Giving Back."

The Significance of the Whaleback Montane

The Whaleback Montane has been characterized as the largest relatively undisturbed representative landscape of the montane section of the Rocky Mountain natural region in Alberta. Indeed, it is possible that this piece of montane is the largest, most intact montane landscape left in Canada. As has been mentioned above, this landscape is unusual in the richness and variety of plants and animals that make their home here.

Montane landscapes are rare in Alberta; they account for less than two per cent of the land area in the province. Most of them are located in major east-west river valleys leading out of the mountains, and as such, are heavily affected by the presence of roads, railways, towns and industrial activities that tend to concentrate in river valleys. The existence of a large piece of montane landscape basically without roads and relatively wild is a great treasure. That this land is still connected to surrounding wild areas makes it even more valuable.

If we wish to retain this precious place for ourselves and those that come after us then it is necessary that we respect and take care of this land. It is also necessary for us to work collectively to ensure that the best possible decisions regarding present and future uses of it are made. To guard against the Whaleback being "loved to death" it is imperative that all visitors respect the land and leave

Ross Hastings at the southern end of the Bob Creek Ecological Reserve.

little trace of their passing. The following chapter in this book: "Safety and Etiquette" details the practices that should be followed by all visitors to this area to remain safe and to avoid damage to the land and its inhabitants.

To ensure that the land is not abused through inappropriate use by individuals, companies or government without an ecological conscience, those that know and love this place should make their voices heard when it is threatened. The final chapter of this book, "Giving Back," contains information on past and ongoing efforts to preserve the region. Please consider joining with the people doing this vital work by supporting the activities of the Friends of the Whaleback, The Alberta Wilderness Association and the Canadian Parks and Wilderness Society. Addresses and phone numbers are listed on page 92.

Grasslands at the southern end of Whaleback Ridge. The Gap is in the centre of the picture on this page.

Early Inhabitants

There has been very little archaeological work done in this area. Most of what is known about the early human occupation is inferred from sites elsewhere. One of the major routes postulated for entry of human beings into North America during the last ice age is along an "ice-free corridor" along the Eastern Slopes of the Rockies. If this corridor existed (its existence is a subject of controversy) it probably went right through the Whaleback area. It is possible that people were camping in this area from the earliest times of human occupation of North America.

The Whaleback is home to magnificent Douglas fir.

It is almost certain that humans have been hunting and camping in the Whaleback area for thousands of years. We do not know with certainty which modern First Nations people these hunters were ancestral to, but there is no reason to doubt that the Piikani (the tribe of the Blackfoot who now have their nation at Brocket near Pincher Creek) have been here a long time. There is some Piikani oral history of this area, especially as it relates to the mythical figure Napi or Oldman. In Piikani culture Oldman is seen as a creator and is identified strongly with various landscape features.

There's a story that goes that Napi the Oldman.... See, that's where he lived all the time and that's why this stream went by the name Napi. Our language says "Napi Taa Taa," that's the Oldman River. There's a place there where they say that Napi was gambling with the Man, I think, from the Mountains. It's said that this other person had hoops, that's what he had, throwing them so far, rolling them.... That's around the Gap, you know. And Napi, Old Man, was getting beat. Somehow he managed, whatever he was bidding, like, all the different birds were his property, he was bidding some and he was losing them, finally somehow he managed to get them all back—he won them back.
Paul Smith, Piikani Elder—Interview November 1996

Aside from the mythic stories that tie Piikani people to this land, there are actual accounts of events with some mythic overtones.

There's another story that goes there (*the Whaleback area*). Our people were camping, my grandfather ... by the name of Bad Boy, his wife, they were on horseback, they were hunting along the hills—elk, moose or whatever. So they seen the herds and my grandfather got one of them. See, they were both on horseback. His wife must have been young in those days, they killed one. And I guess he told his wife: "You stay here, start skinning that animal. I'll follow the others." I guess they went over a hill. He followed them. His wife had his horse, you know. She was hanging on to his horse and saddle. You know, in those days women used to ride just like a man. While she was working some of the Kootenays came along and picked her up. They took her away with his horse. I guess they brought them over the mountains—kidnapped— and there was my grandmother. I guess she was put under the care of an old Kootenay woman wherever they were camping. She was lonesome, she wanted to come home. So when the old lady that was looking after her heard this, she pitied her. She told her: "I'm gonna send you home. But I'll prepare some moccasins and food." Now, that pemmican is an expensive food from way back and I ate some. It's meat—dried meat—sun cured or wind cured and the old people—the old women, would crush it into dust, add fat ... in those days it was deer fat or moose or whatever. Then they're mixed up. That'll stay for days or years, it's preserved, sun cured. I guess she had some of that. The old woman told her: "I'm gonna show you tonight. I'll bring you so far then I'll tell you which way to get out of the mountains." And she was only too glad to obey this woman. I don't know how long that night she had prepared the moccasins, the food. They started and nobody noticed. After a few days and a few nights they didn't think she was going to try to get away. Well, anyway,

An ancient limber pine on Little Whaleback Ridge.

the old lady brought her at night. They went all night to a certain place. She told her from here on you sleep, go in the bush during the day, but at night you walk.... I guess while my grandmother was walking one night a bear came from the bush. And this bear—she [my grandmother] was helpless, she didn't know what to do, so she just gave up and let the bear do what she would. The bear went ahead of her. And she just went up right to the bear and went on alone. I wonder how far she went—the bear got up and passed her again. She just sat down three or four times. Finally she thought, "Maybe he wants me to ride him." That's when she got on the bear and the bear took them out of the mountains to where they were camping. They were still watching out for her. She came one morning on foot to the camps. See, this is our

spiritual help. Our people, our own spirits. There's the oldest spirit of the creator but these are our own spirits.

Paul Smith, Piikani Elder—Interview November 1996

By 1880 the buffalo were nearly extinct and the Piikani were starving. Able-bodied hunters who could travel went to Montana in search of the last herds. Those that didn't leave were reduced to snaring gophers for food. The only food available were the rations given out on the reserves. This effectively removed the Blackfoot from the area. Without buffalo grazing, the grass would have grown quickly.

It didn't take long for the newly dominant European culture to take advantage of the energy stored in this grassland. The pastures the bison once roamed proved very attractive to cattlemen. The Walrond Ranch (later known as the Waldron) was one of the first big ranches established in Alberta and drove in its first herd of cattle in 1883. The ranch covered about 260,000 acres of leased land or over 400 square miles, much of it in the Whaleback area. The first general manager of the ranch was Dr. Duncan McEachran, the dominion veterinarian; most of the capital came from the English upper class. McEachran was against settlers and had many feuds with those that tried to settle on Walrond land. The Walrond was a successful operation throughout most of the 1880s and 1890s. The disastrous winter of 1906 caused it to go into a decline and most of the land was sold off soon after. In the 1960s much of the land was reassembled as the Waldron Grazing Co-operative. The Waldron now owns or leases most of the southern half of Whaleback Ridge. Some of the original ranch buildings are visible just west of the junction of Highway #22 and secondary Highway #520.

Other ranchers took up the leases the Walrond Ranch had held. For most local residents ranching was, and still is, seen as the best way of life for this area. Many of their descendants still run cattle operations in the Whaleback area. Prominent among these are the Blades, Cross, Davis and Nelson families. The fact that the land is still largely unbroken and has large portions without road access is a consequence of the strong ranching tradition that is still maintained in this area.

Until very recently life did not move too quickly in these parts. As Sid Marty notes of his "recent" move to the area: "This is a place where you are still a newcomer after 10 years of residence. They will have to see how your grandchildren turn out before they consider you tenured." Highway #22, which used to be a local gravel road, has been paved. It now sees hundreds of cars an hour at peak times. The travelling time from Calgary has been reduced to the point where urban people are considering "developing" this landscape.

These entwined pressures of increased access to the country by many people and increased pressure to subdivide and sell ranching land for residential or recreational use are the raison d'être for this book. Unless we act now to protect the special unroaded places that are left it will be too late. It is essential that those who know a wild place firsthand, who come to love and respect it by travelling through it, seek to protect it from degradation and destruction. I hope that those who read this book and follow the trails described will take a stand against the kinds of development that would rob us all of this precious landscape forever.

A sacred landscape is one that people connect with, draw power from and feel love for. They know the country and the country knows them. "The country knows. If you do wrong things to it, the whole country knows. It feels what's happening to it." Lavine Williams, Koyukon Elder, 1975

Safety and Etiquette

Land Ownership

The land has remained in its relatively undisturbed state owing, in large measure, to the management practices of the resident ranchers. For this reason alone, it is important that people wishing to walk in the area respect the wishes of the people who live and work here.

There are four types of ownership and control of land in this area:

- **Private Land**—The owner has title to the property. Anyone wishing to enter private land should receive permission from the landowner first. The owner has the legal right to ask anyone trespassing to leave.

- **Leased Crown Land**—The land is leased to the rancher and she/he may exercise some control over the activities of people on the land, especially as their activities may affect operations for which it is leased. The most obvious example of this would be a disturbance to cattle by people on a grazing lease. Generally speaking, the public should have foot access to public rangeland when cattle are not present or when their activities will not disturb cattle. However, the following advice from A. J. Kwasniak, an expert in public lands law, is useful: "A cautious member of the public who is not sure whether his or her entry would disrupt grazing operations, would ask the leasee."

- **Forest Reserve**—Land so designated is Crown land managed by the Alberta Forest Service. The regulations governing what activities are allowed in the area are contained in the Porcupine Hills-Livingstone Integrated Resource Plan. At present (January 1997) there are no restrictions on where or when members of the public may walk in the Forest Reserve area.

- **Ecological Reserve**—This is an area of about 30 square kilometres in the northeast part of the area that is managed under special regulation by the Alberta Forest Service. Walking is allowed in the reserve but overnight camping is forbidden.

Access Considerations

In this region there are few fences and few indications as to the status of the land you are travelling across. The routes described in this guidebook are all located on leased Crown, Forest Reserve or Ecological Reserve land. If you happen to encounter a leaseholder or their agent and are asked to leave the area it is probably wise to do so in an expeditious manner.

One of the most uneasy moments I experienced in this area was in the Forest Reserve near the mouth of Jackknife Coulee. I was approaching a gate on the main trail when I realized that the cow standing on my side of the gate had a rather too alert and dangerous air about it. Instead of running away as I approached, this animal turned full on and faced me. Something in his eyes (by this time I'd ascertained it was a bull and not the usual steer or cow) caused me to back up slowly and, when about 50 metres up the trail, beat a hasty retreat. If a kindly rancher had informed me that there were bulls in the pasture, I would have been glad to turn back earlier.

Leaseholders may sometimes have legitimate management reasons for wanting the public kept out of an area for a limited time. If, however, you are turned away consistently or in what seems to be a capricious fashion, you may want to alert the Alberta Wilderness Association (see page 92 for their address and phone number). The controversy over Crown land access in Alberta will probably not be resolved soon. Leaseholders are likely to be much less resentful of people who attempt to minimize their impact on the land and who are considerate of ranchers' concerns.

$\mathcal{C}$attle

The Whaleback area is home to over 2,000 cattle during the summer months. The vast majority of them are yearling steers (animals castrated as calves) and they are quite shy and spooky around people. The best course of action is to stay as far away from these animals as possible. If you end up on a trail with some of these animals being herded in front of you, you may want to stop for a break to let them get out of the way. Another alternative is to make a wide detour around the animals if possible. What should be avoided is pushing a group of cattle into a corner of a fence or place where they may bunch up, panic and possibly hurt themselves. Some of this area is used to pasture cows and bulls. Bulls should be given a wide berth whereas behaviour with cows is similar to steers, i.e., avoid herding or chasing them.

Cattle left on the open range are subject to a variety of hazards. Chief among these is poisoning by larkspur or locoweed. If you come across an animal that appears in distress or is behaving erratically, do not go near it. By giving it lots of room you will avoid further stress that it would experience if it tries to flee. If possible, you might stop at the nearest ranch house and inform the rancher of animals in trouble.

There are structures in this area that are necessary to the grazing operations being conducted here. Corrals, salt frames, range riders' trailers and cabins are some of the things you may see when travelling in this country. These should

Steers are quite curious but should not be approached too closely.

be left strictly undisturbed as the ability and safety of the riders to do their jobs could be compromised if things are damaged. Likewise it is important to avoid damaging fences and to leave all gates as you find them.

Livestock rustling (stealing cattle) has become a problem in this area. All suspicious activity should be reported to the RCMP at Crowsnest Pass—phone (403) 562-2866 (24 hours). Poaching of wild animals is a similar concern and should be reported to the following toll-free number: 1-800-642-3800. It is not wise to approach suspected rustlers or poachers directly. Get a description of people, equipment and vehicles—license plate numbers are very handy.

Wild Animals

Just as there are hazards from domestic animals, there are safety and conservation concerns for wild animals. One of the major concerns for many people is bears. In the Whaleback area bears come in two types: black and grizzly. Bears are large animals that are equipped for, and sometimes do, prey on other animals for food. In areas where there is a fairly persistent human presence and food and garbage are strictly managed, such as the Whaleback, black bears do not pose much of a threat.

Bears may, however, become human-food conditioned through getting

Grizzlies may not be the most welcome company in the Whaleback. Photo Don Beers.

access to people's food or by people feeding them. This may occur directly or indirectly. Indirectly human food conditioning occurs through throwing food away or storing it where bears can get at it. When camping, be sure not to store food in your tent or anyplace where a bear can get it. Food should be stored by being slung from a tree at least three metres from the ground and well out from the tree trunk.

Cattle mortality because of larkspur poisoning or other natural events does occur in this area fairly often. This poses a problem regarding bears for people travelling in this area. Both black and grizzly bears will come from long distances to scavenge carcasses. This becomes dangerous if a grizzly is surprised

28

on a carcass. At such times anyone approaching may be challenged and possibly attacked. If you see or smell a dead animal, immediately move away from it and make whatever detour is necessary to avoid the area around the carcass.

Recent research into the effectiveness of pepper type spray bear repellents indicates that they are reasonably but not 100 per cent effective in discouraging grizzly bear attacks where it is feasible to use them. A strong breeze blowing into the direction you are spraying renders them useless or worse—you may end up spraying yourself! The best course of action in grizzly country is still that of following behaviours that minimize the chance of a confrontation between you and a bear.

Most bears do not wish to associate with humans. If given enough warning they will leave the scene long before you can see them. This means that in places where visibility is limited and you think a bear may be present you should make sufficient noise to notify a bear that you are in the area. Yodelling, yelling or whistling loudly are quite effective ways of alerting bears to your presence. The sound from "bear bells" does not seem to carry far enough to allow bears to hear you coming before they can actually see you.

The specific behaviour that you should exhibit if you are unfortunate enough to surprise a bear that does not wish to flee varies from situation to situation. For a detailed description of how to lower the chances of a dangerous encounter with a bear and what options are available in such an encounter, consult: *Bear Attacks: Their Causes and Avoidance* by Dr. Stephen Herrero.

Other animals that should be given a wide berth are: cow elk or moose in calving season—usually the month of June, and bull moose in the fall. At these times these normally shy animals can be quite unpredictable and dangerous to approach.

Approaching any wild animal (including birds, reptiles, insects or spiders), should be done with extreme caution. This is primarily a safety issue, both for you and the animal. By approaching too close to an animal you are triggering its "flight or fight" response. This response and subsequent action uses the animal's energy and can weaken its chances for survival if it is living in marginal conditions and its overall energy budget is close to being balanced. In winter this is especially true for many animals. For example, elk can fail to survive a winter if the snow is too deep and the weather is too cold, even without human interference with their grazing.

In the same vein, animals that are reproducing and raising young are very susceptible to disturbance. Nests and den sites should be avoided, not approached. Some birds are so sensitive to disturbance that if driven off a nest even once or twice at particular periods in their nesting cycle they will abandon their nests. Large carnivores such as wolves and wolverines are also very sensitive to disturbance during denning season and may abandon their den site or young if approached too closely. Even small animals will defend their young or themselves if they feel threatened, so it is best to leave them well alone and avoid unnecessary pain both for you and them.

Recent research into human-induced impacts on large carnivores in the Rocky Mountains show that animals such as bears, wolves, cougar, lynx and wolverine can be displaced from their territory by relatively small increases in human activity. This occurs because there are thresholds of disturbance beyond which an animal cannot adjust. If an animal is already stressed by current human activity, then these thresholds may be exceeded by seemingly trivial incidents and the animal will move to a less optimum habitat. To avoid exceeding these thresholds it is important that all people who come into contact with large carnivores give them as much space as possible and do not harass them in any way.

Ticks

Ticks are arthropods that can carry dangerous (but rare) diseases such as Lyme disease and Rocky Mountain spotted fever. Ticks are present in many regions of Alberta and the Whaleback is no exception. There is an excellent pamphlet available about Lyme disease published by Alberta Health and Alberta Forestry, Lands and Wildlife called *Lyme Disease An Alberta Perspective* written by Dr. J. M. Pybus. It recommends that "Those spending time in tall grass, brush or forested areas should shower and make a thorough daily check of the body (particularly head, neck and groin regions) for ticks…." This pamphlet also contains clear, concise recommendations for avoiding ticks and removing them if they do become embedded in your skin.

Pets

All of the situations and arguments regarding human behaviour around cattle and wildlife apply equally to people's pets. If you bring your dog to this area it is imperative that it be under your control. In most cases this means on a lead. It is a rare dog that will refrain from chasing a snowshoe hare, ground squirrel or skunk that springs up from under its nose just because its owner says "No." In the eyes of many ranchers in the area, the best option is for people to leave their pets at home when visiting this area.

Hunting Season

Hunting season peaks from the last week in October until the middle of December. During this time there are hundreds of hunters in this area. There is added personal risk to hikers at this time of year and if you decide to visit during hunting season you should wear bright colours and make your presence known. There is also hunting for bears from April 1 until May 15, and black bear and sheep in September and October. These seasons do not have the numbers of hunters that the peak has, but hikers should take precautions.

Plants

Some plants in this area can be hazardous. The biggest hazard is poisoning from eating mushrooms or berries that are mistaken for an edible species. Unless you are very familiar with the different varieties of wild plants that are edible, it's a good practice to avoid eating any plants found in the wild. Another reason to avoid eating plants here is that very often wildlife depends on the same plants humans consume for their survival. That quart pail of wild raspberries you take home to make into a pie could go to giving a black bear a bit more fat for hibernation and an easier winter and spring.

The same logic applies to picking quantities of wildflowers. Flowers are a resource, both for people who may hike the trail after you and for animals that may use them for nourishment. Flowers are also the precursors to seed pods for plants and if too many are picked then reproduction in that area is affected or an animal's food source may be removed.

Some plants can cause a painful rash if brushed against. In Alberta the two species that are most commonly a problem are stinging nettle and poison ivy. I have seen no poison ivy in this area and there is none reported in the biophysical reports for the area. Nettle is prevalent near the streams in the aspen woodland on the east side of the Whaleback Ridge and is probably found in similar situations throughout the area. If possible, patches of nettle should be avoided entirely, especially if you are in shorts.

Fires

Cutting of live trees for firewood is not acceptable and stoves are the preferred option for cooking. If you do decide to have a fire in this area it should be in an already existing fire ring on an already used site. Appropriate sites are recognizable for having most of the vegetation removed around the fire ring and are common in many parts of this region. Make sure that you burn the charcoal in the fire as fine as possible and put the fire out thoroughly. Dismantle other firepits in the immediate area and scatter their ashes so that subsequent users will employ only one place in a site.

If you cannot find an existing ring on an already used site you should either use a fire pan, construct a mound fire or as a last resort, make a pit fire. Make sure that you remove all traces of your fire if you have had it where there was no fire previously. Siting of fires is critical to recovery of the location. Only mineral soil (soil without organic matter in it) or rocky locations should be used. Ashes should be carefully scattered and the site camouflaged so that it will not be used again.

Travel

The lowest impact form of travel in the backcountry is, in most cases, walking. Cases when walking results in substantial impact to the environment usually involve too large a group of people or people who act without regard for the land they are walking on.

Generally, people walking over most areas of this landscape should be able to leave little or no trace of their passing. There are no hard and fast rules for low-impact walking. There has been extensive research on the effects of recreational walking done by various government agencies in the United States and Canada.

The National Outdoor Leadership School (NOLS), a private non-profit school located in Lander, Wyoming, has done extensive work and published several books on low-impact wilderness travel. The most well-known work on this topic is probably *Soft Paths: How to Enjoy the Wilderness without Harming It* by Bruce Hampton and David Cole. Readers interested in a more

This party of over 100 people left tracks in the grass that were visible three months later.

in-depth explanation of low-impact backcountry practices are urged to consult this or similar works.

Most of the routes in this guidebook follow pre-existing tracks and trails. When on these already heavily-disturbed routes, it is important to stick to the trail as much as possible. Obstacles on the trail such as muddy and wet areas, snowbanks and downed trees should be crossed directly, where at all possible, rather than skirted around. This will confine the impact from walking to the portion of trail that is already vegetation free.

In areas where there is no obvious trail, walking lightly means not contributing to the formation of one. Parties of walkers should spread out over the land as much as possible and avoid walking single file. "Select a route that avoids fragile areas, particularly wet areas, unstable slopes and areas covered by dwarf shrubs or dense broad-leaved herbs and ferns. These are the most fragile types of vegetation and a few passes by hikers will cause lasting damage."

Vehicles

Motorized vehicles, especially motorbikes, tend to gouge deep long-lasting ruts in grassland and forest. To a lesser extent bicycles can be responsible for this type of damage. Motor vehicles driven over dry grass can ignite an unwanted fire through the heat from their exhaust systems. All the people interviewed in the preparation of this guidebook—ranchers, area residents, government agency officials and representatives of conservation groups—felt strongly that there should be a vehicle access management plan for the area. At the very minimum it was felt that vehicles should be restricted to existing major routes such as the track up Camp Creek. The majority view was that vehicles of any kind should not be allowed off the roads maintained by the municipalities. When hiking in this area please park your vehicles at the access points indicated in this guide and walk from there.

Special Places 2000, a government of Alberta protected areas program, will likely be designating a portion of this region a protected area in 1997 or

Off-road-vehicle tracks can take years to heal.

1998. Once this designation is in place a management plan will be implemented for the protected area. This will probably include a vehicle access management plan. Visitors should watch for changes to access points and should be aware of all signs posted.

Party Size

To avoid impact to the countryside and overwhelming other visitors to the area, party size should be kept below 10 people. Four to six person parties are generally recommended as a maximum for most wilderness areas.

Family Matters

In comparison to the adjacent Rocky Mountains, the Whaleback Montane offers a gentle yet scenic landscape to walk through. Portions of routes without much elevation gain on good trails are the lower Bob Creek and Beaverdam Creek trails. Travelling a few kilometres up these trails and retracing your steps would provide an experience characteristic of the area.

Planning a trip into this area with children or older people is similar to planning any trip into a wilderness area. The level of preparation and flexibility of agenda required for safe, successful trips is much higher when taking individuals with limited stamina, energy levels and varying interests and attention spans. It is of critical importance that people unused to wilderness travel not be separated from the group. It is also important that sufficient clothing, food and emergency gear be carried on walks of any length.

There are excellent books that describe in detail how to organize and enjoy wilderness outings with children. Two that seem especially complete and well written are: *Wilderness with Children: A Parent's Guide to Fun Family Outings* by Michael Hodgson and *Starting Small in the Wilderness* by Marilyn Doan.

Footwear

Most of the walking in this area is over relatively gentle terrain. In dry weather running shoes or light hiking boots with some ankle support will be adequate for most trails. If the weather is wet or there is snow on the ground a more waterproof pair of boots is advised. There is generally no need for a deep lug or rigid sole boot on any of this terrain. If you are camping it is a good idea to carry a pair of light moccasins or sneakers for use around the campsite.

Camping

The Whaleback area, as described in the introductory section of this guide, is quite small. The amount of this land that is rare montane landscape on Crown land is even smaller; about 100 square kilometres. Should there be camping in the Whaleback area? Most of the people interviewed felt that random small group (less than 10 people), low-impact camping was the best alternative for the northwest (subalpine) corner of this region and was an appropriate activity there.

There were two main groups of opinion about camping in the montane. One group felt that any camping should occur only in designated areas at access points, e.g., Maycroft Campground and at the A7 access if proper facilities were put in place there. The other group felt that low-impact practices could allow for a level of random camping without leaving impact. In the grassland areas, the montane landscape is quite resistant to damage and could sustain a degree of low-impact random camping without much degradation.

However, I believe that camping is not generally a desirable land use in the montane part of this area. The chance of encounters and conflicts with wildlife or cattle is significantly greater for campers than for walkers passing through this area in the day. Many animals are active at night or early or late in the day. To avoid stressing these animals further it is desirable to limit the times of human presence in this area.

Most of the montane area can be covered by making day trips from the various access points. The areas that are hard to reach in one day are around Jackknife Coulee, Chaffen Ridge, Horseshoe Ridge and Chimney Rock. With the exception of Chimney Rock these areas fall outside the montane and are in the subalpine subregion. Camping in these subalpine areas is likely to result in damage to vegetation so campers should look for already heavily-used sites and camp there.

Serviced Camping

People who wish to camp in a serviced campsite have three choices adjacent to the Whaleback area. On secondary Highway #940 there is a Forest Service campsite at Dutch Creek about five km north of the junction with secondary Highway #517. Farther north there is the Upper Oldman campsite two km west on the Oldman River Road. This road is 9.5 km north of the junction of secondary Highways #940 and #517. The Maycroft Campground is located in an old gravel pit at the junction of Highway #22 and secondary Highway #517.

Other Accommodation

At present (January 1997) there is only the Whaleback Ridge Bed and Breakfast operating at the A7 ranch house. Reservations are *required* and can be obtained by calling Wayne or Maxine Schlosser at (403) 628-2402.

Getting There

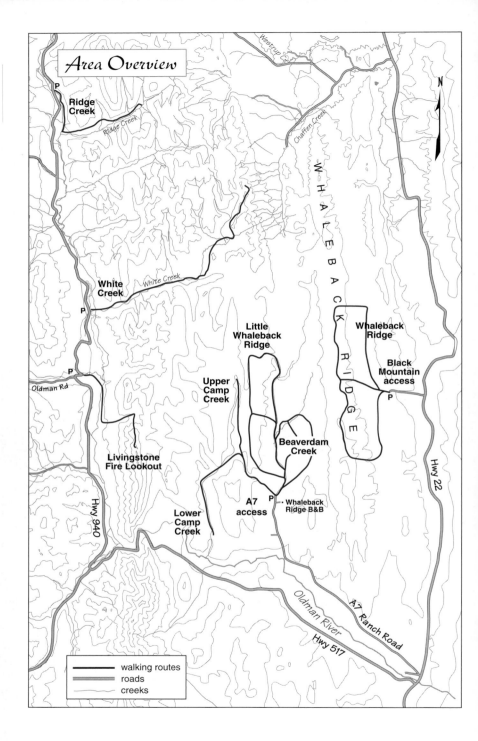

Area Overview

Ridge Creek

Ridge Creek

White Creek

White Creek

Oldman Rd

Livingstone Fire Lookout

Hwy 940

Westrup Cr.

Chaffen Creek

W H A L E B A C K   R I D G E

Whaleback Ridge

Black Mountain access

Little Whaleback Ridge

Upper Camp Creek

Beaverdam Creek

A7 access

Whaleback Ridge B&B

Lower Camp Creek

Oldman River

Hwy 517

A7 Ranch Road

Hwy 22

N

walking routes
roads
creeks

38

How to Access the Whaleback

From the North–Highway #22

The closest access to Calgary is the Black Mountain access about 140 km southwest of the city via Highway #22, which has been called the most scenic road in Alberta. It is probably the most used route into the region. The perspectives it offers of mountains showing their grandeur while at a comfortable remove are unusual and breathtaking.

Leaving Calgary travelling south on Macleod Trail follow Highway #22X west toward Priddis. Turn south on Highway #22 toward Turner Valley. Travel through Turner Valley and Black Diamond turning south at the Black Diamond Hotel. You may, alternatively head south on Highway #2 and drive to Black Diamond via Okatoks. The next and last place to buy gas and supplies on this route is the town of Longview.

From Longview continue south past Chain Lakes Provincial Park. From the hill just beyond the turnoff to the park, the northern end of the Whaleback Ridge is visible in the southwest.

The junction of secondary Highway #520 and Highway #22 is 27.5 km south of Chain Lakes. The hills on the right side (east) of Highway #22 are the Porcupine Hills. The large conifers covering most of these hills are Douglas fir, a tree that is characteristic of most montane landscapes in Alberta.

The arrow indicates the north end of Whaleback Ridge as seen from Highway #22.

Whaleback Ridge from the cattleguard at the Black Mountain access.

Black Mountain Access

From the junction of Highway #520 and Highway #22 proceed 3.9 km south on Highway #22. There is a turnoff and narrow dirt road leading up the side of a coulee on the west side of the highway. This is the *Black Mountain access*. Drive two km up this track and park at the first cattleguard. *Do not block the road. You will require a vehicle with a fairly high clearance and the road may not be passable when wet. This access is located on leased Crown land and is part of the Waldron Grazing Co-operative.*

A7 Ranch Road and Access

Continuing beyond the Black Mountain turnoff it is 16 km to the *A7 Ranch Road*. Turn right (west) and then bear right along the A7 Ranch Road. (If you cross the Oldman River you have just missed the turnoff!) The country changes in a very noticeable fashion in the 16 km between the Black Mountain turnoff and the A7

Ranch Road junction. Dense Douglas fir forests give way to a broad expanse of prairie extending to the southeast. The land on both sides of the highway is owned by the Waldron Grazing Co-operative.

The Waldron also own the land on either side of the A7 road to the cattleguard 5.8 km from the junction. After crossing this cattleguard you are travelling through land owned or leased by the rancher living in the first house on the road located eight km in from Highway #22. If you wish to cross the open land on either side of the road in this stretch from 5.8 to 10 km in you should seek permission at this house.

At the 10 km point the road crosses Bob Creek. The land is owned or leased by the A7 Ranch from this point until you reach the Forest Reserve. The *A7 access point* is located at the end of the road 13.5 km west of Highway #22. Park just beyond the fence where the gravel ends. Take care not to block any gates or roads when parking.

Chimney Rock Road

The northern edge of the Whaleback area is bounded by the Chimney Rock Road. This road appears to be an attractive access into the area. However, appearances are deceiving in this instance. The land on both sides of the road is fenced and much of it is private land posted with "No Trespassing" signs. There is no easily identifiable access into the Whaleback area from this road.

Forestry Trunk Road Access

Just south of the Highway #22 bridge across the Oldman River is Maycroft Road, secondary Highway #517. Turn right here and drive west 22.5 km through the Livingstone Gap to the Forestry Trunk Road, secondary Highway #940.

Livingstone Fire Lookout Parking

From the junction of secondary Highways #517 and #940 head north 9.5 km to the junction with the Oldman River Road. On the way you will pass the Livingstone Ranger Station, Helitack Airport and the Dutch Creek Campground. Turn right at the Oldman River Road and park about 100 metres up the road where it forks.

White Creek Parking

Four km north of the Oldman River Road on secondary Highway #940 there is a pullout opposite the White Creek valley mouth that is visible east of the road.

Ridge Creek Parking

About 17 km north of Oldman River Road on secondary Highway #940 there is a bridge across the Livingstone River. Park just north of the bridge.

From the South
Highway #3 and Highway #22

Travelling Highway #3, drive about 24 km west of Pincher Station to the Highway #22 junction just beyond the town of Lundbreck. If you are coming east from the Crowsnest Pass area, the Highway #22 junction is about 18 km from Bellevue, just beyond the Lundbreck Falls turnoff.

Travel north for 27 km on Highway #22 to the Oldman River bridge. The *A7 Ranch Road* is just over the bridge and the *Black Mountain access* is a further 16 km north of this. See the above descriptions of these access points.

Route Descriptions

How to Use this Guide

Each of the route descriptions in this chapter follows the same format. The *title* is meant to be descriptive of what dominant features the route follows or has as its goal. The *walking time* is a very rough estimate of the time a reasonably fit adult would take to walk over the route. This time does not include any stops except short rests for food. If you are travelling with children or people who do not walk fairly rapidly then you should increase this time. The *elevation gain* is an estimate of how much elevation is gained between the lowest and highest point on the walk.

There is a brief description of how to find the *access* point. For a more detailed description of where access points are located see the chapter "Getting There." *Route descriptions* contain directions on how to follow the route as well as some of the plants, animals and landscape features to watch for.

There are no trail markers of any kind in this area. Some of the routes do not follow any tracks for a portion of their length. Though the country is generally open, it is a good idea to carry a topographic map and know how to read it when hiking here. The appropriate maps are Maycroft 82G/16 for the southern (majority) part of the region and Langford Creek 82J/1 for the northern section. The six digit numbers in brackets in the route descriptions are the UTM (Universal Transverse Mercator) co-ordinates of the feature being described to an accuracy of about 100 metres. The first three numbers are the easting. It can be found directly from the light blue numbers printed horizontally across the map. The first two digits are printed, the third digit you estimate as the number of tenths. For example, 935 is found midway between the blue numbers 93 and 94. The last three numbers are the northing. The procedure for finding the appropriate reading is the same as the easting except you look at the blue numbers running vertically up the map. By finding where the northing crosses the easting you have the position on the topographic map. See the diagram below for examples.

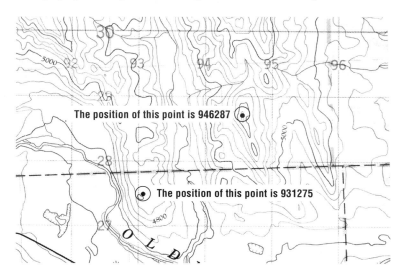

The position of this point is 946287

The position of this point is 931275

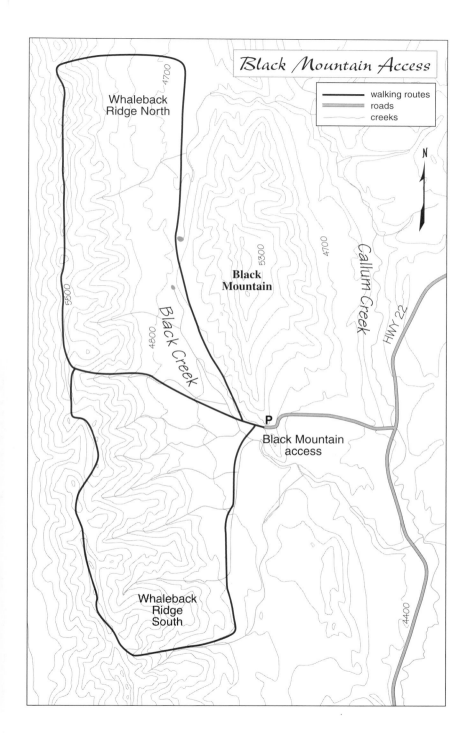

Black Mountain Access

walking routes
roads
creeks

Whaleback Ridge North

Black Mountain

Callum Creek

HWY 22

Black Creek

P
Black Mountain access

Whaleback Ridge South

Whaleback Ridge North

Walking Time—7 hours for full loop, 4 hours for loop to Ecological Reserve
Elevation Gain—about 375 metres (1,200 ft.) plus there is quite a lot of up and down following the ridge.
Access—Park at the Black Mountain access—the road is 4.2 km south of the junction of Highway #22 and secondary Highway #520. Park at the highway turnoff and walk the road approximately two km to the first cattleguard on the south shoulder of Black Mountain. If you are driving a vehicle with high clearance and the ground is dry you can drive the first two km of this road to the cattleguard.

"Ecological Reserve"—what an evocative title. I feel like I did the first day I went to the zoo. I was five years old. Today is the day I get to see the Ecological Reserve. The hike in to the boundary is wonderful, with awesome views and wildflowers everywhere. Not much sign of wildlife, but surely when I get to the reserve there will be more. Two-and-a-half hours of steady walking gets me

Wildflowers on the slopes of Black Mountain.

to the fence. And that's all there is, a fence and a sign. The country is the same on both sides of the fence. No herds of elk or deer shelter in this reserve. And there are cowpies in there too. From the first hill I can see across to the western boundary of the reserve. I realize this reserve isn't that big and it doesn't seem that special. Later, I learn that in this ecological reserve hunting and grazing are permitted activities. What isn't allowed is overnight camping. So, in reality this is a sort of no camping zone. All in all a bit of a letdown.

At this point you are looking west at the Whaleback Ridge. This is about the midpoint of the ridge, which is about 30 km long. In this area there is a transition from closed forests interspersed with meadows to an open prairie containing patches of forest. The dense stands of Douglas fir and white spruce mixed with aspen that dominate the landscape in the northern part of the region shift to a more open savanna of rough fescue grassland with open patches of Douglas fir, limber pine and aspen that is characteristic of montane landscapes.

This walk leads through a wide diversity of ecotones reflected by an astonishing array of different plants. Late May through June sees the whole area covered with the blossoms of innumerable wildflowers, providing a rich tapestry of colour laid across the hills. Only a few of the many species of plants and animals to be seen on this walk have been listed in this description.

The views from the ridge top are well worth the effort to climb up.

47

Shooting stars are a common wildflower in this area.

Route Description

From the shoulder of Black Mountain walk down the road to the WNW past the junction to the road that leads south (028358). Watch for old man's whiskers and buffalobean on the slopes beside the road. This area has many Columbian ground squirrels. Their predators, red-tailed hawks, Swainson's hawks and occasionally, golden eagles, will be seen gliding and soaring over these open slopes. Mammalian predators that are common in this area are badgers and coyotes.

Where the road turns north about half a kilometre farther on cross the small creek (025359) straight ahead (WNW) and follow the cart track WNW toward a prominent coulee leading up to the Whaleback Ridge. This trail passes under the powerline ascending through groves of aspen situated between bogs rich in a variety of wildflowers and shrubs. This 500KV powerline was routed through this valley in 1985 despite the strenuous protests of the Alberta Wilderness Association and other conservation groups. *Stay on existing paths and avoid trampling delicate vegetation in wet areas when walking in this area.*

The trail crosses a small creek near an old beaver dam and enters the mouth of the coulee (009364). Watch for shooting stars, wild geraniums and violets as you go through this area. The slope to the right is south facing and supports large patches of balsamroot, which in late May and June make vivid splashes of yellow that contrast beautifully with the bright purple lupines that also flower on these slopes.

Ascending the coulee in late May and June you may notice extensive patches of forget-me-nots and false solomon seal where snow collected at the bottoms of gullies and the coulee. The slope on the left of this coulee as you ascend is a dense forest of spruce and Douglas fir. Cow parsnip and baneberry are common along the creek leading up the coulee.

This may be the most northerly blue camas in Alberta.

Near a small pond, about two thirds of the way up the ridge, the trail takes a turn to the south (002365). A gully ascends to the north. Follow this gully up to the ridge crest (000369). Awesome vistas await those walking this crest on a clear day.

The bedrock that is exposed along the ridge crest is coarse-grained, light gray sandstone of the Upper Cretaceous Belly River Formation. On this ridge grow wind-flagged limber pine and Douglas fir, showy Townsendia, heart-leaved arnica, bearberry and creeping juniper.

There are two obvious exit trails from the ridge as you travel north along its spine. The first occurs at the southern boundary of the Upper Bob Creek Ecological Reserve (000379) where an obvious road leads back into Breeding Valley and a road leads south back to Black Mountain and the parking spot. The length of this option is 3-1/2 to 4-1/2 hours.

Secondly, if you wish to make a full-day hike and experience a complete transition to closed Douglas fir forest continue along the ridge through the Ecological Reserve. Follow the trail along the fence line, this provides the best path through what is otherwise heavy undergrowth. Along the way a number of hillocks along the spine of the ridge will be ascended and descended. After descending approximately 75 metres (250 ft.) into a major notch (998407) you will see an obvious track crossing the ridge. Follow this east, descending through a large patch of cow parsnip into a dense forest of Douglas fir. This trail descends into Breeding Valley where it passes some very large specimens of Douglas fir near the valley bottom. Continue on this trail passing under the powerline again and connect with the old exploration road running along the east side of the valley.

This road leads past a number of ponds with an interesting variety of plants. Watch for blue camas and sweet grass in moist places near the edge of ponds and streams. A wide variety of birds and animals live in this valley. In the summer waterfowl such as teal and mallards are common, as are bluebirds and other songbirds. Ungulates, including elk, whitetail deer, mule deer and moose are abundant.

In the fall many hunters use this valley. Wearing bright colours and making some noise as you travel is advisable. Leave all gates as you found them.

Whaleback Ridge South

Walking Time—5 hours
Elevation Gain—about 375 metres (1,200 ft.) plus there is quite a lot of up and down following the ridge.
Access—Park at the Black Mountain access—the road is 4.2 km south of the junction of Highway #22 and secondary Highway #520. Park at the highway turnoff and walk the road approximately two km to the first cattleguard on the south shoulder of Black Mountain. If you are driving a vehicle with good clearance and the ground is dry you can drive the first two km of this road to the cattleguard. This hike takes place mainly on Waldron Ranch leased Crown land. Please make sure you give any cattle plenty of room and leave gates as you find them.

There is a certain magic in some places. Places that are known to be good for healing attract people from far away. The energy in other places is sometimes patently sensuous. Walking through meadows overflowing with the scent and colour of innumerable wild blossoms we were beguiled by the fecundity of July. The day was hot; I could see the sweat glistening on my companion's legs. We stopped on the ridge, breathless with the exertion, the heat and the beauty surrounding us. It was a perfect place for a meal and blissful dreams.

Bob Creek valley and Livingstone Ridge from Whaleback Ridge.

Walking this route takes the hiker from prairie through creekside willow communities into aspen woodlands then climbs into Douglas fir-limber pine forests. Walking along the ridge is challenging in places but the variety of plant communities and the changing vistas make the effort worthwhile. This section of the Whaleback Ridge overlooks some of the most dramatic landscapes in the region.

There are many places along this ridge that merit stopping and soaking up the unique spirit of the place. Even if the day is warm and the flies are annoying there is usually enough breeze to keep the open ridge bug free.

Some of the ridge top is pleasant and open.

Route Description

The start of this route is the same as for Whaleback Ridge North Loop. When you get to the point ascending Whaleback Ridge where the coulee and road diverge (002365) turn south and follow the road up to a saddle on the ridge crest.

Go east then south from this point (002360) following the ridge crest. The broad grassy valley you're overlooking to the west is Bob Creek valley. To the east the Porcupine Hills dominate the horizon with Black Mountain prominent in the foreground. As you follow the ridge it takes a jog to the west about a kilometre from where you first reach it. The best course here is

to follow the largest game trail. After descending about 100 metres there is a pond in a saddle (003351). Look for blue-eyed grass, ground plum and shrubby cinquefoil in this area.

The route continues on or parallel to the ridge line. Walking is quite rough with a lot of up and down. Finding a game trail that's going south and staying on it at times seems preferable to staying on the ridge crest. Continue this way for about two km beyond the pond. At a major saddle with a barbed wire fence corner in it (009328) there is a valley leading off the ridge to the southeast. Descend this valley on game trails. Watch for false hellebore, wild vetch and wild strawberry when going down this valley.

After about half a kilometre there is a trail junction marked by a salt block holder (017328). Continuing down the valley on the now well-defined trail leads to a junction with a cart track running along the valley (026330). Turn north (left) and follow this road back through the willow patches and grasslands to the parking spot at Black Mountain.

Spruce cone

53

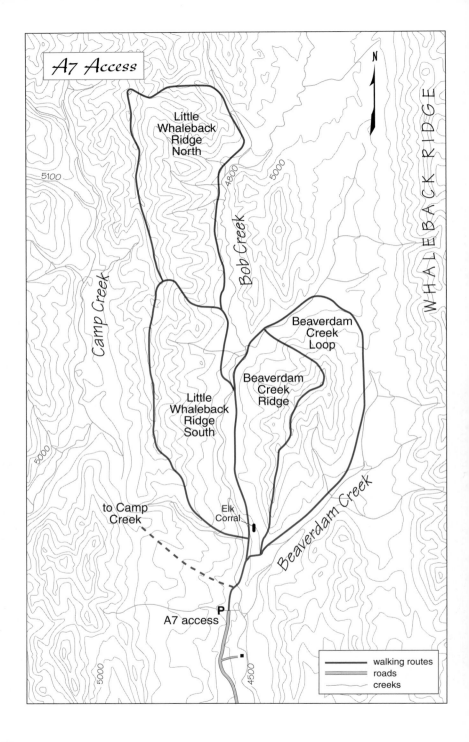

A7 Access

Little Whaleback Ridge North

Bob Creek

Camp Creek

5100

4800

5000

WHALEBACK RIDGE

N

Beaverdam Creek Loop

Beaverdam Creek Ridge

Little Whaleback Ridge South

5000

to Camp Creek

Elk Corral

Beaverdam Creek

A7 access

P

4500

5000

	walking routes
	roads
	creeks

Little Whaleback Ridge South

Walking Time—5 hours
Elevation Gain—about 300 metres (1,000 ft.) and there is a bit of up and down along the ridge.
Access—Park at the A7 trailhead located just beyond the cattleguard about one km past the A7 Ranch buildings (972296).

Many people have now heard of the Whaleback. They may have seen a poster or even a video of the place. But the reason that there's been so much publicity is not visible on this thundery day. We walk past the site of the proposed Amoco test well and climb up to the ridge sweating, breathless. At the crest, a dramatic scene awaits, curtains of rain sweep between us and the nearby Livingstone Ridge. Soon the squall is upon us and we are getting wet. Still, our smiles do not falter as we follow the ridge crest, the country spread out below. We see no one else the whole day and we hear only the sound of the wind, and smell only the scent of rain-soaked Douglas fir and grass. We return with our boots wet and our souls washed clean.

Looking down (south), Camp Creek valley from Little Whaleback Ridge.

Cottonwood forest along lower Bob Creek.

This walk takes the hiker through many of the vegetation categories present in the Whaleback area. The trail initially travels through a riparian cottonwood area. It then ascends into grasslands interspersed with willow communities, and ascends again through aspen woodland into ridge top limber pine and Douglas fir. Finally the route descends through broad south-facing ridges of grassland.

There is a wide diversity of scenery with vistas of rolling grass and tree-covered hillsides side by side with awesome views of the front ranges of the Rocky Mountains visible right into Montana. Many species of birds and animals frequent this area and it is not uncommon to sight deer, elk, coyotes, Clark's nutcrackers, hawks and eagles while on this walk. People with sharp eyes may see signs of, or actually observe other animals such as black or grizzly bears, cougars and badgers, and birds such as blue grouse, lazuli bunting and pileated woodpecker.

Route Description

Cross Bob Creek at the ford up the road just north of the access and follow it along the east side of the creek. There is a junction (974303) with a trail leading

east over a small ridge to Beaverdam Creek. However, continue straight north up Bob Creek valley to the elk corral. This round corral was built in the mid 1980s to enable elk to be caught and transported to other parts of Alberta where they were being reintroduced.

Along this section, from the parking area to the elk corral, the trail passes through riverbank (riparian) cottonwood forest. The principal tree species present are balsam poplar and western cottonwood. Narrowleaf cottonwood has also been reported in this area. Some of the shrubs found here include wolf willow, rose, red osier dogwood and saskatoon.

Leaving the corral the trail climbs on a terrace of open grassland. Many prairie flowers bloom here throughout the spring and summer including prairie crocus, showy locoweed and yarrow. This grassland is interspersed with patches of aspen woodland. There are also several springs beside the trail in this area that are ringed by willows.

Aspen groves and Douglas fir on Little Whaleback Ridge.

It is in this area that AMOCO Canada Petroleum proposed to drill an exploration well in 1994. Permission to drill this well was denied by the Alberta Energy Resources Conservation Board after an extensive public hearing. (For a fuller description of the events and issues surrounding oil and gas exploration and development in this area see the last chapter.)

The trail passes into the Forest Reserve (970330) and then crosses Bob Creek at a ford a few hundred metres farther on. There is no discernible difference between one side of the Forest Reserve boundary and the other, and in July and August you are as likely to encounter cows in the Forest Reserve as outside of it.

The effects of aspect and soil condition (depth and wetness) are quite noticeable in this area. On this side of the creek fingers of Douglas fir forest extend about halfway down the north side of the Little Whaleback Ridge buttresses. Extensive patches of aspen are present on the lower fringes of these extensions while south-facing slopes of the ridge buttresses are grass covered. The Douglas fir do well in the dry, thin rocky soils that characterize the ridge top while the aspen favour the richer soils deposited farther downslope.

Continuing along the trail you pass the junction of Bob Creek and a side valley leading northeast. Whaleback Ridge forms the eastern horizon looking up this valley. A little farther along the trail goes through an aspen grove. Where the trail emerges from this grove (969342) there is a junction with a trail leading off the main track that goes up a grassy slope to the northwest. Ascend this trail through groves of Douglas fir and meadows of wildflowers to the crest of the ridge (959346). At this point you are looking west over Camp Creek valley (locally known as Spring Creek). The Livingstone Ridge dominates the western skyline and the Livingstone Fire Lookout should be plainly visible.

Take the track that leads south along the ridge. This ridge consists of about 2.5 km of amazing vistas, slopes covered with wildflowers and ridge tops crowned with gnarled limber pine and Douglas fir.

While walking along this crest you are likely to see ruffed grouse, blue grouse, Clark's nutcrackers and Canada jays. In the summer Swainson's hawks, red-tailed hawks and golden eagles can be seen circling near the ridge. Mammals are somewhat more difficult to see but you may see signs of badgers, coyotes, bears (black and the occasional grizzly), elk and mule deer. Look for the mounds made by the northern pocket gopher and for the burrows of Columbian ground squirrels.

The grasses on this ridge include various types of fescue and oat grasses. Other common plants include bearberry, juniper, shooting star, geraniums, forget-me-nots and asters.

The ridge crest ends (960320) overlooking a broad grassy ridge that slopes down to the southeast. As you descend this ridge you will see the trees change from Douglas fir to aspen groves. Noticeable among the many varieties of grasses and flowers growing on this slope are extensive patches of prairie sagewort. In places where snow drifts in the winter there are patches of buckbrush growing.

After a little over a kilometre the slope ends at the edge of a forested creek valley running west-east (972306). Follow this edge east down to Bob Creek. Cross the creek and rejoin the main trail in the vicinity of the elk corral. From this point it's about a kilometre south to the A7 access.

The Forest Reserve boundary on the Bob Creek trail.

Little Whaleback Ridge North

Walking Time—8 hours
Elevation Gain—about 360 metres (1,200 ft.)
Access—Park at the A7 trailhead located just beyond the cattleguard about one km past the A7 Ranch buildings (972296).

"I think I need a good workout. I'm tired of going out with people and coming back still full of energy and wanting to have done more." This was Cathy's answer when I asked her what kind of a hike she would like.

The day started on an exciting note. We were walking up the Bob Creek trail not far from the car when we saw a line of tracks in the dust. Close examination revealed them to be bear tracks; not just one set but two. A mother and cub. The mum's looked pretty big to me and they looked too fresh for comfort. "What were they doing here?" we asked ourselves as we followed them up the road.

The ridge top is classic limber pine-Douglas fir savanna.

Our question was answered by a foul smell. A dead cow lay beside the creek. We detoured as widely as we could and continued.

The first two hours of hiking seemed to only whet our appetite for more. By the time we had climbed the ridge, walked along for several kilometres and descended we were ready for home. But how far was it? We were in upper Bob Creek valley and it was getting late. The prospect of running across Mama bear and her cub in the dark did not thrill us. So we hoofed it for home as fast as we could. We arrived back at the car just after the sun set. It was a beautiful evening. The stars shone like jewels as it got darker. On the way home we stopped at Chain Lakes and our necks got sore looking up in awe at the Milky Way. It felt good to be alive.

Upon gaining the crest of Little Whaleback Ridge this trail goes north about three km before turning east and descending into Bob Creek valley. Along the way the terrain changes from open limber pine-Douglas fir forest to dense stands of spruce and lodgepole pine. When travelling this route you are walking from the montane into the subalpine. Crossing this transition between landscape

Large Douglas fir on ridge.

The trail descends through dense stands of lodgepole pine and white spruce.

subregions gives the observant walker plenty of opportunity to observe a great variety of plants and animals in diverse situations.

Landscape changes are dramatic on this route. Descending from the ridge into Bob Creek valley takes the hiker from windy, exposed open ridges into the protected hushed bottoms of deep valleys. Returning to the access along Bob Creek allows close views of willow communities that gradually change to riparian cottonwood forests. This is a walk that consists of contrasts and shifts of landscape. By noting these changes while walking it is possible to achieve an understanding of the larger context of the montane landscape and its connection to surrounding ecosystems.

Bob Creek looking north.

Route Description

The start of this route is the same as for Little Whaleback Ridge South Loop. Upon gaining the crest of Little Whaleback Ridge (959346) turn north and follow the ridgeline.

Ascend the ridge through a very open limber pine-Douglas fir ridge top forest. Rock outcroppings along the ridge are light gray Upper Cretaceous sandstones from near the base of the Belly River Formation. Looking west you are overlooking upper Camp (Spring) Creek valley. The valley leading west from Camp Creek is Jackknife Coulee. Looking northeast you are looking into upper Bob Creek valley and the Whaleback Ridge beyond.

The difference in vegetation looking east and then west from the ridge is striking. East, there are ridge top forests of Douglas fir and limber pine surrounded by aspen groves and grasslands on the lower slopes and valley bottoms. Looking west you are looking into dense forests of spruce and lodgepole pine extending up to the rocks of the Livingstone Range.

Along this ridge top the dominant grass is Parry's oat grass with substantial amounts of fescue and bluegrass present as well. Flowers commonly found along this ridge are tufted fleabane, death camas, wild gaillardia and bluebells. As you travel north along the ridge large specimens of Douglas firs are encountered.

After travelling along the ridge for about three km you will come to an obvious trail leading west (954376). A few hundred metres farther on there is a major trail leading east. Descending this trail you will pass through thick Douglas fir forest and then into heavy stands of lodgepole pine mixed with white spruce. The understory here includes alders, Canada buffaloberry, wild raspberry and thimbleberry.

After descending for about 1.5 km the trail intersects a small creek (966377). A few hundred metres farther on the trail branches; follow the *left* branch along the creek. This trail meets the main trail coming up Bob Creek about one km from the junction (972369). Turn south (right) at this point and follow the Bob Creek trail about seven km back to the A7 access. The descent of Bob Creek gives the walker a close view of dense willow communities that grow along the creek. Watch for moose and mule deer in the willows and for beaver in the stream. Flowers to be seen on this section of trail include tall larkspur, goldenrod and red paintbrush.

Beaverdam Creek Ridge

Walking Time—4 hours
Elevation Gain—300 metres (1,000 ft.)
Access—Park at the A7 trailhead located just beyond the cattleguard about one km past the A7 Ranch buildings (972296).

My introduction to this route was tumultuous. I arrived at the A7 access to see many cars and trucks parked in the trees and on the grass. It soon became apparent that there were dozens of people camped here. Not only that but there were lots of dogs, very noisy, howling dogs. I had stumbled on a full scale hound trial. This group was very well organized and had set up portable latrines and a camp kitchen and organizational tent. After they moved out there was very little trace of their presence left.

Still, the trials were being conducted in the Forest Reserve in the Beaverdam Creek valley and ridge. The noise was indescribable. First a motorcycle would drag a dead animal around a circuit and then a about a dozen hounds were released. Baying madly, they raced up the ridge and then down into the valley, following the scent. The track from the motorcycle and the

Beaverdam Creek Ridge looking west.

hounds was still there two months later when I went that way again. I hope there were no live animals in the area because I'm sure with all the hounds they would have been scared witless if not chased and harassed.

Should a rare and unique landscape like the Whaleback montane be subjected to such use? I know that day I felt invaded and intruded upon by the noise and commotion of this trial. There was certainly an impact from vehicles driving to and from the trial site and from the motorcycle dragging the bait around the course. Any animal capable of moving undoubtedly left the area. It took about half an hour of hiking until I couldn't hear the hounds. I'm not sure where such an event would be appropriate but in this area it felt like a violation.

This route provides the quickest way to get a feel for the Whaleback montane landscape. Though the trail is quite steep in places there are rewarding views on every side to distract the walker from the labour of climbing. The ridge itself is a profusion of wildflowers in June with areas that are blue with forget-me-nots.

Route Description

Cross Bob Creek at the ford up the road just north of the access and follow the trail along the east side of the creek. There is a junction (974303) with a trail leading east over a small ridge to Beaverdam Creek. Take this trail and just beyond the Forest Reserve boundary (975305) there is an ORV trail climbing the ridge line to the north. Follow this trail up onto the ridge crest. Look for umbrella plant, nodding onion and showy aster in this area.

Follow the ridge crest to its summit (985330). From here descend the spur leading to the northwest. Stay on the edge of the trees to the south of the spur ridge. The spur ends in a tributary valley to Bob Creek (978338). The ground is quite marshy here. If possible, cross the creek and pick up the trail on the north side. Go west (left) from here. If the creek is too high or there is too much water in the marshy areas contour around the bottom of the ridge to the west.

Before you reach Bob Creek there is a trail going south (973337). Take this trail across the tributary to Bob Creek. There is a junction with a track leading uphill soon after the creek is forded. Take the lower (west) fork. This trail has many interesting springs on it; watch for animals in this area. Go a little less than a kilometre keeping right at another junction until the trail meets the main trail going down Bob Creek. Follow this trail about three km back to the car.

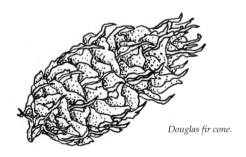

Douglas fir cone.

Beaverdam Creek Loop
(Recommended for Winter Only)

Walking Time—5 hours

In the winter (December-April) many elk graze in this area. They are more easily encountered and spooked when walking the ridges. To minimize disturbance at this time it is a good practice to walk in the valleys. Beaverdam Creek valley is quite wet and marshy in the summer but is more easily travelled in the winter.

Route Description

Instead of climbing the ridge after entering the Forest Reserve continue on the trail leading northeast into Beaverdam Creek valley. Follow this trail as it skirts the eastern edge of the ridge. There are several junctions in the trail, take the left fork at each. There is a good section of sedge meadow (992327) about three km from the Forest Reserve boundary. Look for marsh reed grass, beaked sedge and awned sedge while walking through this area.

After crossing the sedge meadows there is a section of narrow valley with aspen and willow in the bottom and then after about a kilometre and a half the route emerges into the broad prairie that stretches north into Upper Bob Creek Ecological Reserve. This portion of the walk is a great prairie trek. Cross the valley in a

Oat grass is also common in this area.

northwest direction and after crossing a small creek pick up the trail heading southwest into Bob Creek valley. There are two coulees heading north from this trail that make nice side trips if you have the time. (Add another hour or two to your time.)

As you come into Bob Creek valley there is a trail leading south (973337). Take this trail until it meets the Bob Creek trail and continue south to the access.

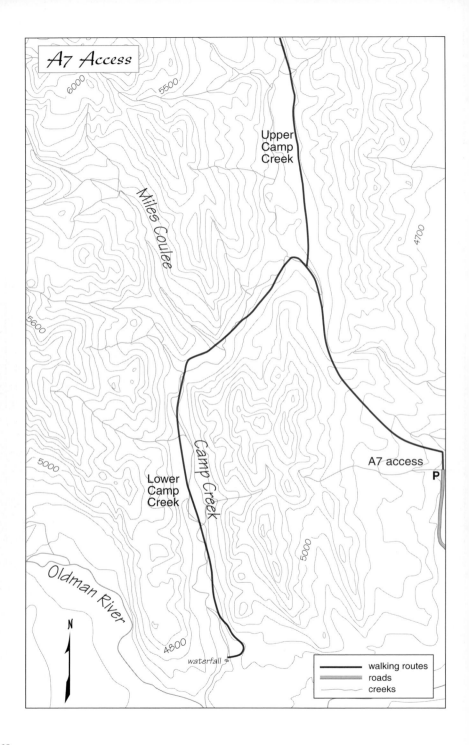

Camp (Spring) Creek

Walking Time—5 hours for either Upper or Lower Camp Creek
Elevation Gain—250 metres (800 ft.)—150 metres going in, 100 metres coming out.
Access—Park at the A7 trailhead located just beyond the cattleguard about one km past the A7 Ranch buildings (972296).

There are some wonderful old Douglas firs on this route. When you come across them in the quiet of the evening their presence is palpable. I was stopped in my tracks by one of these great beings as I crested a hill, plodding, oblivious, back to the car. Something drew my gaze up from the trail in front of me and there was this wonderful old tree radiating peace into the evening. I admired it from a distance for a while as it was so big if I got close I'd lose sight of its form and distinctive character. Then I walked slowly up to it, noting the deep grooves in its bark and places where it had been damaged and had healed. Finally I was close and could smell its sweet scent. The rest was as inevitable as a Harlequin romance. I reached out and caressed the rough trunk and, succumbing to an overwhelming desire, I stepped up close and hugged the tree for many long minutes.

This series of small hills was likely left by stagnant ice melting at the end of the last Ice Age.

The waterfall—Lower Camp Creek.

When I recovered my senses enough to realize where I was, I found that my arms did not go even halfway round this tree! It is about 1.5 metres in diameter and must be hundreds of years old. Long before there were Europeans in this country this tree was here. I realized that with any luck, long after I'm gone this tree will still be here. Maybe some weary traveller will come over this same hill in 2050 AD and be taken out of themselves in the same way I was. If we can value this tree for itself, and not as a commodity with a price on it, then there is a chance that it'll still be here to beguile and amaze others with its ancient presence.

This relatively flat walk leads the visitor into the meadows of Camp Creek (known locally as Spring Creek) valley. These meadows occur in the transition zone from montane to subalpine vegetation and there are many interesting "edges" for the observant traveller to explore.

Route Description

From the A7 parking spot there is a trail leading up the hill to the northwest just before the Bob Creek ford (972298). Climb this hill to the Forest Reserve boundary (958305). After crossing this boundary the trail enters a Douglas fir forest and goes over a saddle into Camp Creek valley. Look here for hairy wild rye, pine grass and northern bedstraw. After coming out into open grassland the trail comes to a junction in Camp Creek valley (952321).

The Douglas fir.

Lower Camp Creek

The trail leading south (left fork) goes down Camp Creek for about five km before meeting with the main trail running parallel to the Oldman River. The trail crosses Camp Creek and its tributaries several times so be prepared for wet feet if the water is high. Initially the trail passes through streamside willow communities, occasionally crossing meadows of fescue grassland or passing through aspen groves. The kilometre or so of the route north of the Oldman trail is a very pleasant walk through meadows on benchlands above a riparian cottonwood forest.

Rough fescue grasslands are common in this valley.

The trail meets another trail descending from Miles Coulee (934308). Go south here to continue down Camp Creek. Continuing south there is an Alberta Forest Service campsite (937286) and about a kilometre south the trail crosses the Forest Reserve boundary (939278).The junction with the Oldman trail is about another kilometre south on the rim of Camp Creek valley (943272). Descending the Oldman trail into the valley is worthwhile as there is an attractive waterfall just downstream of where the trail fords Camp Creek. Return the way you came from this point.

Limber pine cone.

Upper Camp Creek

From the junction (952321) take the north fork along a series of grassy benches to the east of the creek. After about two kilometres there is a field of small hills (probably kames) in the valley bottom to the west of the trail. North of here the vegetation starts to change from Douglas fir dominated montane to plants characteristic of subalpine landscapes.

The trail now starts to go through fairly dense forests of spruce and lodgepole pine. After about three km of travelling along the valley bottom there is a major junction (370944). This is the place to turn back if doing an average day trip. The fork to the left goes north into the White Creek drainage. The one to the right ascends the Little Whaleback Ridge and then descends into Bob Creek valley as described in the Little Whaleback Ridge North route description.

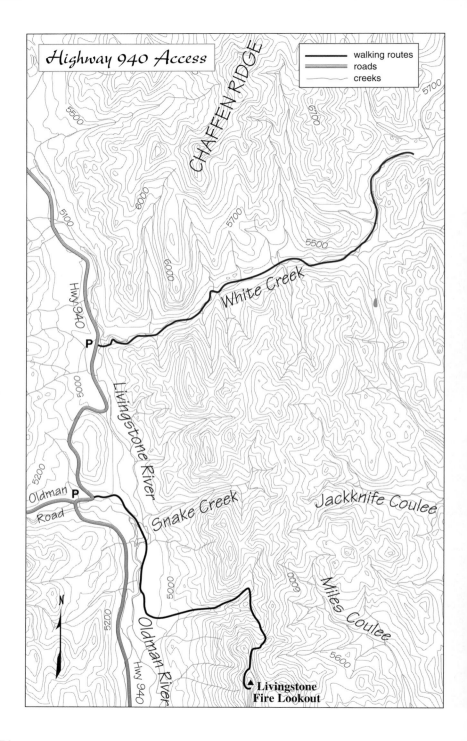

Highway 940 Access

walking routes
roads
creeks

CHAFFEN RIDGE

White Creek

Hwy 940

Livingstone River

Snake Creek

Oldman Road

Jackknife Coulee

Miles Coulee

Oldman River

Hwy 940

N

Livingstone
Fire Lookout

Livingstone Fire Lookout

Walking Time—6 hours
Elevation Gain—700 metres (2,300 ft.). This is a straight up and then down route.
Access—Turn right off the Kananaskis Highway (secondary Highway #940) at the junction with the road going along the upper Oldman River. Park at the first fork about 100 metres from the junction. The route follows the road to the right.

I was camping for several days at the Oldman River campsite. The campsite is quite beautiful; nestled deep in the valley it is well protected from the strong winds that often blow here. However, after a time I became somewhat claustrophobic. The sound of chainsaws cutting trees nearby usually awakened me at dawn. I decided to see what was really up in the country. What better observation point than the fire lookout.

The scene from this lookout is at once heartbreaking and hopeful. On the west side of the Livingstone Range the view encompasses the Upper Oldman and Livingstone River valleys right to the British Columbia border. It is stupendous-looking mountain country where every valley and forested hillside is scarred with a network of logging roads and clearcuts. The landscape looks dissected and fragmented as if a corpse had been thrown down on a table and cut up and its vital organs removed.

Looking east the view is radically different. The Porcupine Hills constitute the horizon of what at first glance appears to be an undisturbed landscape. The patterns of vegetation on the Whaleback Ridge and the other ridges that sweep up to the lookout are full of curves and lines that follow the contours of the land. The logic of glaciers, chinook winds and the angle of the sun is plainly visible on the land. It is only when you look closely that the few fine lines of the seismic cuts and the off-road-vehicle trails become noticeable. I can hear the rending and tearing going on right now in the Oldman Valley just below my feet. The thought of this type of destruction crossing the ridge to disfigure the sensuous, wild landscape of the Whaleback fills me with horror.

The Livingstone Fire Lookout perches on the crest of the range that divides the montane landscape of the Whaleback from the subalpine landscape of the Upper Oldman and Livingstone River. The contrast between the rugged grandeur of the dense forests and bare stone of the High Rock Range to the west and the grassy open hills of the Whaleback country is pronounced.

The strong connection between the Whaleback area and the lands to the west can be clearly seen looking north along the ridge to the White Creek and Ridge Creek valleys. These valleys run east-west against the predominant north-south grain of the mountains and foothills. For the herds of elk and other wide-ranging animals that call this area home these valleys are important migration routes to and from the winter pastures of the Whaleback.

The traces left on the land by the glaciers of the last Ice Age are plainly visible from here. The U-shaped valley of the Oldman River that stretches southeast to the broad prairie and the rounded hills of the Whaleback and lesser ridges are evidence of the power of moving ice. This hike allows the observant person to see the large landscape-scale components and processes that are integral to making the Whaleback the unique place it is.

Clearcuts west of the lookout.

Route Description

From the parking place walk down the right-hand road keeping on the main trail for about 1.5 km to a ford of the Livingstone River (873356). **This ford is often knee deep even in midsummer and could be dangerous at high water.** A few hundred metres beyond the ford the trail meets a new logging road running along the east side of the Oldman. This road is being used to extend clearcutting into the Snake Creek valley just north of this point.

Turn right (south) and follow this new logging road for about two km to a junction with an old road leading east (874338). Follow this old road up through a pleasant mixed aspen lodgepole pine forest. About one km from the junction there is a gate across the road. Near here are a few Douglas fir marking the western boundary of the montane in this area.

The trail climbs steeply and steadily from this point onward. It parallels a creek for much of its ascent and in places the understory of the lodgepole pine and spruce forest is quite dense with alder and willows. This is good bear country and it would be prudent to make a fair bit of noise when travelling through this area. In addition to the common subalpine flowers such as paintbrush, glacier lilies and blue clematis walkers should look carefully for various orchid species in the wetter areas near the trail.

After climbing for about three km the trail emerges at an exposed saddle (899331). The headwater valley of Miles Coulee is the major valley that drops away to the east from here. Montane landscape elements such as limber pine and Douglas fir are visible on the ridge leading south from this saddle. The final section of trail leading up to the lookout is steep, but views are revealed on both the west and east

Cow parsnip is a common plant in shaded locations.

side of the ridge. The ground is studded with many types of wildflowers including mountain avens, alpine anemone and common saxifrage.

The lookout is only staffed from the beginning of May till about mid June. The views are stupendous from here and it is well worth the while to spend some time examining the lay of the country for evidence of geologic, climate and weather related influences on landforms and vegetation patterns. For this area the lookout is as close to an aerial view as one can get without actually getting on an airplane.

The return route is a straightforward retracing of the route in. It should take less time than getting up as it's all downhill, but I find it takes me as long to get back out as going in. Maybe those walkers with stronger knees and higher pain thresholds will reduce my estimated walking time.

White Creek

Walking Time—6 hours
Elevation Gain—150 metres (500 ft.)
Access—Park just off secondary Highway #940 about 3.5 km north of the junction with the Upper Oldman Road (864394). Ford the Livingstone River (knee deep in midsummer) below its confluence with White Creek. Climb up to the benchland above the river until the trail is intercepted. Turn left at this point.

White Creek is just deep enough to have some fish. For many years I've been fascinated by the world under the water, sometimes visible to us but untouchable. In White Creek at midsummer the water is so shallow and clear that you actually feel you could reach down and touch the beautiful cutthroat trout that lie in the shadows. At the end of several hours walking I find myself watching the trout, my mind drifting

Conglomerate outcrop on upper White Creek.

down, being swept along like the mayfly.... Suddenly there's a silvery rush and a splash and I wake with a start; the mayfly disappears into a sparkling swirl. What a beautiful kill, as lovely to my eyes as a lion taking down a gazelle. Vibrant pulsing life and swift death are very near us at all times. Refreshed, I rise and start the long walk home.

This is a basically a flat hike up the bottom of a broad creek valley. There are numerous fords (over a dozen) so walking in footwear that is comfortable when wet is recommended. On a hot day this is a nice walk to do in rubber soled synthetic sandals and shorts.

Route Description

The route starts in a lodgepole pine-spruce forest. The steep-sided canyon of lower White Creek is on the right. This area is rather wet and poorly drained. Watch for horsetail, twin-flower and veiny meadow rue along this section.

Lower White Creek looking west.

The trail fords the creek about 1.5-two km from the Livingstone River. There are two more fords soon after and then the valley begins to open up into grassy meadows (891406). About 1.5 km farther west the trail fords the creek again. Tree species here are predominantly lodgepole pine, spruce and aspen.

This hike is tied closely to the creek. As you walk along it and cross it you will notice various birds and animals that depend on water. Look for dipper, belted kingfisher and cutthroat trout. Also present in the water are a wide variety of invertebrates such as stonefly nymphs and caddis nymphs.

After a series of fords the trail forks (920412). The fork to the south (right hand) goes over a low ridge into the headwaters of Camp Creek. Take the left-hand fork (west) up the White Creek valley. The trail soon turns north and enters an attractive treed valley. After walking about one kilometre up the valley the trail passes an interesting conglomerate outcrop. The creek goes through a series of rocky chutes here and the spot has an interesting air about it. Return to the parking spot by the same route.

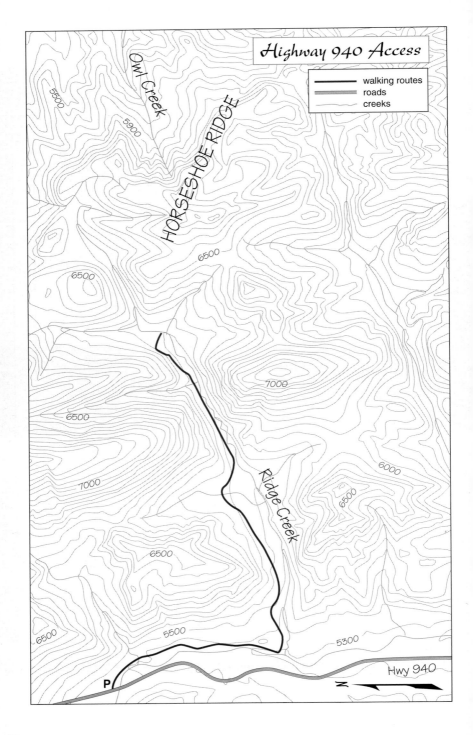

Highway 940 Access

walking routes
roads
creeks

Owl Creek

HORSESHOE RIDGE

Ridge Creek

Hwy 940

P

N

Ridge Creek

Walking Time—4 hours
Elevation Gain—120 metres (400 ft.)
Access—Park off secondary Highway #940 north of the bridge across the Livingstone River, just south of the Livingstone Falls Campground.

Sometimes it's important to try your resolve against something. Usually when I feel down or inadequate I find a good physical challenge successfully met can reaffirm my faith in myself. However, in the mountains the law of the country is you will only go where and when the conditions let you. One day as I walked up Ridge Creek feeling rather low, I found my gaze drawn to the heights of the ridge that looms over the northern end of the valley. The closer I got to this ridge, the more I wanted to climb it.

When the trail passed right under the base, I started up. At first it was lodgepole pine, steep and thick, and difficult to go forward unless on a game trail. There were plenty of those here—there must be lots of moose, deer and elk in this country. Higher up, the subalpine fir and Engelmann spruce make little groves in steep meadows. Still, I can see the rocky ridge crest high above.

There is some aspen in the Ridge Creek valley.

The western horizon, which I could not see until I climbed out of the valley, is ominous looking. Black clouds trailing curtains of rain are sweeping across the High Rock Range. The distant rumble of thunder vibrates the air and a faint breeze, where before it had been still, fans my sweaty face. How long do I have? Can I make the ridge and get down far enough before the lightning comes? Ah, the delicate balance between desire and danger. It is one good reason to come to the mountains.

In the end I push on up to the ridge as fast as I can, heart thudding painfully against my ribs, breath rasping in my throat. I look over and gaze into the northern Porcupine Hills. Beautiful. I turn to the west. The sky is filled with black clouds and the wind is gusting. The curtains of rain are obscuring the Livingstone Valley now and the thunder is loud. Time to go!

Leaping as fast as I dare down the heavy scree I can feel sideways rain come into my face and eyes. I start thinking maybe I've left it too late. Suddenly on my left a small gully appears leading straight down off the ridge. I duck into this and miraculously it's calm. The ripping noise over my head is the gale. It's not even wet where I am—the water is being blown over me. I descend, and do not get soaked or fried. Half an hour later the sun is out and I'm walking through patches of forget-me-nots so dense that I have to watch every step to avoid crushing any of them.

This trail is a good access route into the high ridge country on the northern end of the Whaleback area. The trail itself makes an easy, pleasant day hike. Those walkers with energy and ambition will have many tempting ridge tops beckoning to them from the trail as it wends through the valley headwaters. This trail is entirely within the subalpine landscape and has an interesting variety of plant communities representative of local environments.

Route Description

There is a barbed-wire fence on the east side of the road with a gate in it about 100 metres north of the bridge. Cross the fence here and walk southward down the road through another fence. Continue along the Livingstone River. Another fence is encountered about half a kilometre farther on. This is the last one. Follow the track along the river for about 2.5 km until it turns west up Ridge Creek valley.

Travelling up the valley is very pleasant walking through open lodgepole forest. After about two km the trail goes through a large fen. There is a junction just before this wetland. Take the left fork to keep your feet dry. Walking through this part of the route you are likely to see sweetgrass, Labrador tea and arctic willow.

Higher up the valley the trail passes between the ends of two ridges (875503). From here it continues up the valley into an area of meadows and an interesting side valley. The ridge tops to the north are in the alpine vegetation zone and have some fine specimens of whitebark pine growing on them.

Return to your car the same route you came in on.

Giving Back

Preserving the Whaleback

Background

A little over 100 years ago the Whaleback was merely another part of the great sweep of untrammelled country that stretched from the Rockies to the Red River at Fort Garry (present-day Winnipeg). The area's ecology was in equilibrium with the surrounding country and the human inhabitants of the land. The animals and plants that the area supported were probably the same ones that had been there for millennia. Within the last 120 years much of that has changed.

By 1881 the buffalo that had roamed throughout this area were gone. The people who had depended on them in this area primarily, the Piikani tribe of the Blackfoot Confederacy, were confined to reservations by 1886. As the buffalo declined native hunters turned to other species and by the time the first ranchers settled the country in the early 1880s the land was barren of most large mammals.

The ranchers interviewed for this guidebook expressed the view that they and their ancestors have managed this area as cattle operations for over a century and that in doing so they have effectively preserved the area from the detrimental effects of modern industrial society that have been seen elsewhere in Alberta. To a large extent they are correct in this assertion. The landscape has not been scarred by large-scale logging or mining activities. The vegetation is, in large measure, the same species composition as it was in 1885 and the animals that frequent the area are largely the same ones that used it then. However, three types of action used to promote ranching have had an impact on the land and its inhabitants.

The grass that had sustained the great herds of buffalo is now used to pasture ranchers' herds of cattle. The use of the land by ranchers is very different from that of the Piikani. Native burning of the landscape was a common practice and had contributed to keeping the aspen confined to the wetter areas of the region. With the coming of settled residents and fencelines, fire was seen as a destroyer of property. The value of trees as timber led to a general policy on forested lands of fighting fire. At present, fire control in the area is carried out from the Livingstone Gap Helitack Forest Service Base located in the Oldman River valley. Immediately following thunderstorms in dry summer weather large yellow helicopters cruise slowly back and forth over the Whaleback and the Porcupine Hills looking for lightning-induced fires.

The major result of fire control is that the country is much more treed than it was a century earlier. Land managers reported in interviews that they felt the area was overdue for burning and that prescribed burns or selective logging might be desirable options to prevent a massive wildfire as the result of excessive fuel buildup. Douglas fir is a tree that, when mature, has thick, corky bark that resists grass fires well. The buildup of dead wood and dense stands of Douglas fir over the last 50 years leaves the region vulnerable to very large, hot fires that may destroy much of the tree cover in the area.

In previous years range improvement activities consisted of cutting back aspen growth and seeding the land with various domestic grass species. Horses used to herd cattle, trail ride or hunt are fed domestic hay and the seeds are subsequently spread in droppings. By both of these means non-native species such as timothy, brome and crested wheatgrass have become common in many parts of the region. Another common invader is Canada thistle. This gains a foothold where the ground has been disturbed and cut up by overgrazing, trampling by cattle or stripped of vegetation through actions like road and trail building. Introduced species can out-compete many of the native plants in certain types of sites in this region. A loss of diverse native species can result in a lowering of the ability of the ecosystem to be resilient in the face of changes such as those caused by climate change or fire.

While grazing has not generally had a noticeable impact on the land in most places, one area that does seem to be affected by cattle is that of wetlands, particularly springs. At present cattle are not fenced off from springs or pools in the grazing leases or in the Forest Reserve. The result has been muddy creeks and trampled springs in parts of the region. The Cows and Fish Project (Alberta Riparian Habitat Management Project) has been successfully working with many ranchers in the area to mitigate the damage cattle cause to streamside vegetation.

Trampling of springs interferes with the flow and contaminates the water, making it unfit for humans to drink. Trampling has a negative aesthetic effect. A spring of clear water looks much nicer than a mudhole churned up by countless animals. Finally, any rare or unusual plants that are confined to the area in and around water can be damaged or destroyed by too much trampling.

Another change in species that occurs through management for grazing involves predator control practices. Wolves especially are not tolerated by ranchers in grazing areas. In the early years of the ranches in this area, wolves were systematically exterminated and did not return to the area till the early 1990s. In 1994 there were wolves denning in the area but they were killed later that year as part of a control program. Removal of predators from a system allows prey species, in this case ungulates such as moose, elk and deer, to reach population sizes and concentrations that are detrimental to the existing ecosystem. Uncontrolled population growth may also lead to populations that grow large enough to expand into adjacent areas. In this case elk are a major problem for ranchers adjacent to the Whaleback as they feed heavily on hay both in the field and that stored for winter.

While ranching has resulted in some change in conditions on the land such as those described above,

A trampled spring in Bob Creek grasslands.

on the whole "well managed cattle operations on many of these leased areas have sustained their ecological diversity and natural landscape quality." (Pachal, 1992, p. 27)

Since the late 1960s there have been a series of far more potentially destructive developments proposed for this region. A brief description of these threats to the functioning of the natural processes in the region is described below along with the responses of area residents and environmental groups. As this description will make clear, focussed action by concerned individuals and groups can, in many cases, help preserve a precious landscape. It will also show that more effort needs to be made to ensure that the wilderness values of the area are maintained.

Resource Development

Aside from an exploratory oil well drilled in Breeding Valley in the 1960s and then abandoned, there were very few resource extraction activities undertaken in the region before 1970. However, by the mid 1970s a general resource rush on the Eastern Slopes region of Alberta resulted in *A Study of Park Potential in the Eastern Slopes* published by the Alberta Parks Planning Branch in 1977. The authors of this landmark study, Cheryl Bradley, Lynn Bradley and Jim Gilpin, recommended that most of the area covered in this guidebook be managed as a park.

Their proposal was that this park would be "managed co-operatively by the Fish and Wildlife Division, Provincial Parks Division and the Natural Areas Coordinator of the Lands Division, to provide strong landscape protection and orderly recreational use of this unique area." They envisioned that the area would be divided into a general outdoor recreation zone, a wildland recreation wildlife zone and a natural area zone. Different areas would be managed for the appropriate values with only limited forestry allowed in the White Creek valley. All other extractive uses, with the exception of controlled grazing, would have been disallowed.

The Alberta Wilderness Association (AWA) strongly endorsed the report's acknowledgment that this "is a distinctive landscape unique in Alberta and apparently in Canada" and that "Preservation of the Whaleback area in its relatively natural state is therefore of prime concern...." By 1980 the AWA was deeply involved with the Alberta government's Integrated Management Planning process for preparing the Livingstone-Porcupine Hills Integrated Resource Plan (IRP), which encompasses the Whaleback area. The planning effort was led by an interdisciplinary team composed of representatives from Alberta Forestry Lands and Wildlife, Alberta Energy, Alberta Recreation and Parks, Alberta Environment and Alberta Agriculture. Public input was solicited in 1984.

The Livingstone-Porcupine Hills IRP was completed in 1987. The vast majority of the Whaleback area was zoned "critical wildlife" with the plan clearly stating that: "South of the Chaffen-Bob divide the primary intent is to protect critical wildlife habitat and ecological resources." (Alberta Forestry)

Blue grouse on the south end of Little Whaleback Ridge.

The land north of the Chaffen-Bob divide was zoned "multiple use" with small areas in White Creek, Bruin Creek, Ridge Creek and Beaver Creek valleys zoned critical wildlife. Alpine and sensitive subalpine areas on Livingstone Ridge, Chaffen Ridge and Horseshoe Ridge were zoned "prime protection." This designation is seen as incompatible with industrial and resource extraction activities.

The IRP is a policy document and, as such, has no legal status and can be amended at the discretion of the minister responsible for Forestry, Lands and Wildlife. It is an important document in that it guides how all Alberta government departments act in the region. What the IRP does not do is automatically preclude any proposals for land use and development. The preface to the plan states: "No legitimate proposals will be categorically rejected. The provincial government is committed to serving Albertans; should a proposal not be in keeping with the provisions of the plan, every means will be taken to explore alternative means for accommodating the proposal in a more appropriate location, either in this planning area or on other public lands." The plan is essentially a document to guide development, not to promote preservation.

The tension between development and preservation has been a constant theme in the Whaleback area since 1980. In that year the AWA was an intervener into the Alberta government's Energy Resources Conservation Board (ERCB) hearings on Trans-Alta Utilities' application for an electrical transmission line that would be routed through the Whaleback area. The AWA's intervention objected to the route of this line passing through the Whaleback area. In 1982 the AWA made a formal request to the ERCB that the yet to be built 500 kilovolt transmission line be realigned from its proposed corridor through the Breeding Valley-Big Coulee section of the region to along Highway #22 to the east. This request was denied and the line was erected along the eastern flank of Whaleback Ridge.

Another action that generated controversy in the area was the sanitation logging of limber pine to prevent pine beetle infestation of lodgepole pine, a commercially important species. There is some doubt as to whether the beetle that infests limber pine is the same one that attacks lodgepoles so this initiative may have been unnecessary. This action occurred in 1985, apparently without consultation with the Integrated Resource Planning branch.

Following the publication of the Parks Planning report recommending the establishment of a protected status for the region in 1977, there have been a number of initiatives to achieve this goal. The AWA published its first "Areas of Interest" map and listing in the fall of 1983. It included the Whaleback region as a candidate Wildland Recreation Area, with an Ecological Reserve Core.

In 1986 the AWA published *Eastern Slope Wildlands, Our Living Heritage*. This book was designed to inform the public about 13 candidate areas in the Eastern Slopes, including the Whaleback. Several other reports were generated and delivered to various branches of the Alberta government in the years between 1986 and 1993, including an application to the International Union for the Conservation of Nature (IUCN) for assessment of the Whaleback area as a World Heritage Site.

In 1994 there was a major showdown between development and preservation supporters. The event that initiated this was Amoco Canada Petroleum Company Limited's (Amoco) proposal to drill an exploratory well in Bob Creek valley. The well to be located at 9-18-11-2 W5M would have been in the middle of lower Bob Creek valley, deep within the Montane landscape. Amoco apparently started surveying for this well in May, 1993 before applying for a well license from the Alberta government's regulatory body, the Energy Resources Conservation Board (ERCB, now the Alberta Energy and Utilities Board—AEUB). Visitors to the area noticed the survey activity and contacted the AWA. The AWA asked to be notified as soon as the ERCB received an application to drill.

The ERCB held a pre-hearing meeting on December 14, 1993 to determine the location and time for a hearing as well as the scope of the hearing and the funding for local interveners. By this time two groups had formed to intervene against the proposed well. The Hunter Creek Coalition was composed primarily of local residents while the Whaleback Coalition was a mixture of local residents, and members of the Alberta Wilderness Association and the Canadian Parks and Wilderness Society (CPAWS).

The hearings were held in May of 1994. Much of the testimony focussed on the ecological value of the area and whether these values would be compromised by the well. The two coalitions mentioned above, as well as representatives from the Peigan Nation, the Alberta Nature Federation and the Alberta Fish and Game Association were very direct in their opposition to the well on the basis of it affecting the ecological integrity of the area. The most significant anticipated impact was an increase in vehicle access into the area. These interveners also made the argument that the Whaleback area "clearly represented the largest and least disturbed example of a montane ecosystem in Canada." (ERCB, p. 31)

The board denied Amoco's application. In its decision it stated:

> On the basis of the evidence, the Board found it difficult to accept that Amoco can successfully develop an all-weather road into the Bob Creek valley without causing a significant long-term risk of permanently increasing public access and thereby having an unacceptable impact on wildlife and other values of the area.... The Board also believes that the Whaleback area represents a truly unique and valuable Alberta ecosystem with extremely high recreational, aesthetic and wildlife values. It accepts the position of some interveners that the area is a primary candidate for protection under the Special Places 2000 program.

The result of this government-sponsored enquiry into the use that should be made of this land clearly highlighted its need for preservation and protection.

Special Places 2000

Special Places 2000 is the government of Alberta's protected areas strategy released on March 28, 1995. Many groups (especially conservation organizations) were severely disappointed in the strategy (Kennett), which seemed to favour the interests of "those who feared any additional restrictions on their use of public lands for recreation and profit." (Ibid, p. 2) A boycott of participation on the Provincial Co-ordinating Committee for Special Places 2000 was undertaken by a wide range of environmental groups. The minister of Environmental Protection made some changes in the policy that made it clear that preservation was the primary goal and also announced his personal nomination of Upper Elbow-Upper Sheep and the Kakwa areas to the Provincial Co-ordinating Committee. With legislative changes to the Willmore Wilderness Act pending that would have eliminated motorized access, the Federation of Alberta Naturalists and CPAWS agreed to sit on the committee.

In the midst of this controversy over Special Places 2000 the Alberta Forest Service made plans to issue logging permits for part of the Whaleback area. This impending action was widely publicized by conservation groups and the premier of Alberta "quickly called a halt to the approaching sale of the logging permits and announced that no logging would be permitted in the Whaleback Wildland." (Pachal, 1966, p. 17) Furthermore, the premier also stated in a meeting with the Wilderness Caucus of the Alberta Environmental Network that there should no development in candidate areas while they are being discussed.

The Future of the Whaleback Area as a Protected Area

At this time (January 1997), a large part of the Whaleback area has been recommended by the Provincial Co-ordinating Committee for protected status. The overwhelming majority of people interviewed for this project felt that if the area was to be protected, its status should be similar to Willmore Wilderness, in other words, what is known as a Wildland Park in the Special Places 2000 policy. "Wildland Parks encompass large areas of natural landscape where human developments and interference with natural processes are minimized." (Landals, p. 9) This level of protection does allow hunting, fishing and the use of horses. Motorized recreation, resource extraction and industrial activities are not allowed with the notable exception of controlled cattle grazing. A local committee is being formed to draw up specific guidelines and boundaries for the protected area and will probably take 6-18 months to finish its deliberations.

The Alberta government has stated that existing dispositions (leases) will not be bought out in the Special Places process. For subsurface leases in the Whaleback, there are 11 five year Petroleum and Natural Gas Licences held by five companies, the last due to expire in 2001, four Coal Leases held by two companies, the last due to expire in 2007 and one Metallic and Industrial Minerals Permit due to expire in 2006. The surface activity disposition of greatest concern for preservation is logging. There are two existing logging leases both due to expire April 30, 1997.

The continuing existence of these agreements represents a serious threat to preservation efforts. Any protection of the area would be severely compromised by mining, logging or oil and gas development. Lobbying the government for a policy of not renewing existing leases is an important first step to dealing with dispositions. Negotiations also need to be initiated with lease holders to terminate current dispositions as soon as possible. Options that the province has to offer current leaseholders range from tax reductions to land swaps if it is unwilling to use cash to buy out the dispositions. Lobbying efforts by concerned citizens will be essential to ensuring these actions happen.

Even if the process for designating the Whaleback as a protected area goes smoothly and it is given an appropriate level of protection, there will still be many continuing conservation issues pressing. Chief among these is maintaining the area's connection to other wild areas. For example, many of the elk in this area move between the Upper Oldman drainage and the Whaleback on a bi-annual basis. The need to protect the Upper Oldman area is pressing, as is the need to identify other crucial areas and paths of connectivity between the Whaleback area and surrounding landscapes. The uniqueness of this area depends in large measure on the mixture of species that coalesce here from different landscapes; this blend of species must be maintained to ensure the integrity of the Whaleback.

Organizations Helping to Preserve the Whaleback

In Alberta there are several effective, vital organizations made up of people who are passionate about preserving wilderness and who have involved themselves deeply in activities designed to protect the Whaleback area. If you feel this unique area should be maintained in its natural state, you would do well to work with one or more of the following groups:

Friends of the Whaleback, 9734-88 Avenue,
Edmonton, Alberta, T6E 2P9, Phone (403) 433-7904

Alberta Wilderness Association (AWA), 455-12 Street N.W.
Calgary, Alberta, T2N 1Y9, Phone (403) 283-2025

Canadian Parks and Wilderness Society (CPAWS), 1019-4 Avenue S.W.
Calgary, Alberta, T2P 0K8, Phone (403) 232-6686, Fax (403) 232-6988

Personal Actions

Never doubt that a thoughtful, dedicated group of individuals can change the world. Indeed, it is the only thing that ever does. Margaret Mead

As well as joining or supporting one of the groups mentioned above, there are a number of individual actions that you can undertake if you wish to make a difference in the protection of this area. The most obvious is to tell your family, friends and associates about the Whaleback and about the need for protecting the landscape, both the area itself and the surrounding country.

An effective personal action that can be undertaken on those cold snowy days when the Whaleback should be left to its non-human inhabitants is lobbying. This usually involves writing letters, faxes or making phone calls to politicians who may be in a position to influence the course of events. A short list of provincial politicians concerned with environmental issues in the province of Alberta follows:

The Hon. Ralph Klein
Premier of Alberta
Fax (403) 427-1349

The Hon. Ty Lund
Minister of Environmental Protection
Fax (403) 422-6259

Ms. Debby Carlson
Official Environment Critic
Fax (403) 427-3697

Send all letters to any on the above list to:
The Legislative Building
Edmonton, Alberta
T5K 2B6

Be aware that this list will change with party reorganizations, cabinet shuffles and elections. A complete up-to date listing of relevant Alberta politicians is published in every issue of the Alberta Wilderness Association's quarterly, Wild Lands Advocate. Any of the conservation organizations listed above will provide names and background to issues; contact them for current information.

While on a walk in the Whaleback or surrounding country take pictures of the natural beauty (and also of any humanmade, unnatural ugliness). An eye-catching submission using pictures and words can then be created. Lobbying need not be tedious work, a letter writing party or a salon to discuss conservation issues and assemble a submission can be a great way to get together with friends of like mind.

Some Plants Found in the Whaleback Area

Flowers

alpine anemone	*Anemone parviflora*
arnica, heart leaved	*Arnica cordifolia*
aster, showy	*Aster conspicuus*
balsam root	*Balsamorhiza sagitta*
bluebells	*Campanula rotundifolia*
blue eyed grass	*Sisyrinchium montanum*
blue camas	*Camassia quamash*
blue clematis	*Clematis verticellaris*
buffalo bean	*Thermopsis rhombifolia*
bunchberry	*Cornus canadensis*
cow parsnip	*Heracleum lanatum*
false solomon seal	*Smilacina stellata*
false hellebore	*Veratrum eschscholtzii*
forget-me-not	*Myosotis alpestris*
gaillardia	*Gaillardia aristata*
geranium	*Geranium spp.*
goldenrod	*Solidago canadensis*
ground plum	*Astragalus crassicarpus*
horsetail	*Equisetum spp.*
Labrador tea	*Ledum groenlandicum*
larkspur	*Delphinium glaucum*
loco weed, showy	*Oxytropis spendens*
loco weed, early yellow	*Oxytopis sericea*
nodding onion	*Allium cernuum*
northern bedstraw	*Galium boreale*
old man's whiskers	*Geum triflorum*
prairie smoke	*Geum triflorum*
paintbrush, red	*Castilleja miniata*
prairie crocus	*Anemone patens*
prairie sagewort	*Artemisia ludoviciana*
pussy-toes	*Antennaria spp.*
saxifrage, common	*Saxifraga bronchialis*
shooting star	*Dodecatheon spp*
townsendia	*Townsendia sericea*
twin flower	*Linnaea borealis*
umbrella plant	*Eriogonum spp.*
veiny meadow rue	*Thalictrum venulosum*
violet, bog	*Viola nephrophila*
white mountain avens	*Dryas hookeriana*
wild strawberry	*Fragaria virginia*
wild vetch	*Vicia americana*
yarrow	*Achillea millefolium*
yellow mountain avens	*Dryas drummondii*

Grasses & Sedges

awned sedge	*Carex atherodes*
beaked sedge	*Carex utriculata*
hairy wild rye	*Elymus innovatus*
marsh reed grass	*Calamagrostis canadensis*
oat grasses	*Danthonia spp.*
pine grass	*Calamagrostis rubescens*
sweet grass	*Hierochloe odorata*
fescue grasses	*Festuca spp.*

Trees

cottonwood, narrowleaf	*Populus angustifolia*
cottonwood, western	*Populus deltoides*
Douglas fir	*Pseudotsuga menziesii*
pine, limber	*Pinus flexilis*
pine, lodgepole	*Pinus contorta*
pine, whitebark	*Pinus albicaulis*
poplar, aspen	*Populus tremuloides*
poplar, balsam	*Populus balsamifera*

Shrubs

alder, green	*Alnus crispa*
alder, river	*Alnus tenuifolia*
arctic willow	*Salix arctica*
bearberry	*Arctostaphylos uva-ursi*
buckbrush	*Symphoricarpos occidentalis*
buffaloberry, Canada	*Shepherdia canadensis*
cinquefoil, shrubby	*Potentilla fruticosa*
dogwood, red osier	*Cornus stolonifera*
juniper, creeping	*Juniperus, horizontalis*
juniper, common	*Juniperus, communis*
raspberry, wild	*Rubus idaeus*
rose	*Rosa spp.*
saskatoon	*Amelanchier alnifolia.*
thimbleberry	*Rubus parviflorus*
willows	*Salix spp*
wolf willow	*Elaeagnus commutata*

Selected Bibliography

Achuff, P. L. (1992, July). *Natural Regions and Subregions of Alberta: A revised classification for protected areas management. Report No. 2*. Parks Service and Natural and Protected Areas, Alberta government.

Alberta Environmental Protection Natural Resources Service Parks Support Division Heritage Protection and Education Branch (1995, May). *Alberta's Montane Subregion, Special Places 2000 and the Significance of the Whaleback Montane*.

Alberta Forestry, L. a. W. (1987). *Livingstone-Porcupine Hills Sub-Regional Integrated Resource Plan* (ENR Technical Report Number: T/106). Edmonton: Alberta Forestry, Lands and Wildlife.

Bradley, C., Bradley, L. & Gilpin, J. (1977, June). *A Study of Park Potential in the Eastern Slopes*. Alberta Parks Planning Branch.

Brado, E. (1984). *Cattle Kingdom Early Ranching in Alberta*. Vancouver: Douglas & McIntyre.

Bryan, L. (1991). *The Buffalo People Prehistoric Archeology on the Canadian Plains*. Edmonton, Alberta: University of Alberta Press.

Energy Resources Conservation Board (1994, September). *Application for an Exploratory Well Amoco Canada Petroleum Company Limited Whaleback Ridge Area*. Calgary: Energy Resources Conservation Board.

Hampton, B. & Cole, D. (1995). *Soft Paths: How to Enjoy the Wilderness without Harming It*. Mechanicsburg, PA: National Outdoor Leadership School/Stackpole Books.

Herrero, S. M. (1985). *Bear Attacks: Their Causes and Avoidance*. New York: Nick Lyons.

Jameson, S. (1987). *Ranches, Cowboys and Characters Birth of Alberta's Western Heritage*. Calgary: Glenbow Museum.

Kennett, S. A. (1955, March). *Special Places 2000: Protecting the Status Quo*. Resources: The Newsletter of the Canadian Institue of Resources Law, No 50, 1-7.

Landals, A. (1995, September). *Landscape Biodiversity Preservation Through Special Places*. Edmonton: Alberta Environmental Protection Natural Resources Service, Parks.

Marty, S. (1995). *Leaning On the Wind: Under the Spell of the Great Chinook*. Toronto: Harper Collins.

Pachal, D. (1992). *Wild Alberta*. Edmonton: Environmental Council of Alberta.

Pachal, D. (1996). *Will Promises Become Reality? An Update on Achieving Protected Areas in Alberta*. Wilds Lands Advocate: The News Quarterly of the Alberta Wilderness Association. 4(1), 4-17.

Wallis, C. (1980, January). *Montane, Foothills Parkland and Southwest Rivers: Natural Landscapes Survey 1978-1979*. Resource Assessment and Management Section Alberta Parks Division Recreation and Parks.